Medjugorje
Our Lady Speaks To The World

By
Jerry Morin

Inspired by the apparitions at

Medjugorje

Bosnia, Herzegovina

The author and the publisher recognize and accept that the final authority regarding any reported Marian apparitions rests with the Holy See of Rome, to whose judgment they willfully submit.

Published by *Servants To The World Publications*,
  P.O Box 642 Kirksville, MO 63501. All rights reserved
Publisher email: publisher@medjugorjetotheworld.com
Front cover – Earth – NASA © 1990 used by permission
Front composite cover and interior pictures by Kuhn Productions, Des Moines, Iowa and Jerry Morin
Front cover - "GOSPA, Queen of Peace", original
 painting by Carmelo Puzzolo, 1998. Used by
 permission
Printed in the USA © Jerry Morin 2012 Library of Congress

Medjugorje Our Lady Speaks To The World **book**
ISBN 978-0-9663280-2-8

***Medjugorje - Our Lady Speaks To The World*AUDIOBOOK**
ISBN 978-0-9857464-6-9

Medjugorje Our Lady Speaks To The World **book** with **Queen of** *Peace Messages* **audio CD**
ISBN 978-0-9663280-7-3

Medjugorje Our Lady Speaks To The World E-BOOK (Kindle, Nook, IPAD and most e-support)

Table of Contents

Author/Publisher Page II
Message of the Blessed Virgin Mary 8/16/84 IV
Dedication & Special Thanks V
Invocation to the Holy Spirit... VI
Preface...VII
Chapter 1: Medjugorje 1
Chapter 2: Live The Message - Prayer, Faith,
  Fasting, Conversion, Peace 11
Chapter 3: Message, Scripture & Reflection...................... 23
Chapter 4: Illuminating Messages 79
Chapter 5: Called To Witness.. 91
Novena To St. Joseph.. 110
Chapter 6: The Holy Will and Private Revelation 111
Chapter 7: Blessed John Paul II as Intercessor 116
Chapter 8: Author's Reflection on
  Fatima/Medjugorje.. 119
Chapter 9: Facts and Quotes to Ponder............................ 125
Chapter 10: Medjugorje Updates 129
About the Author... 132
Servants To The World Mission....................................... 133
Author's Fruits of Medjugorje 134
Bibliography and Endnotes... 137

"Dear children, I beg all of you….to live my messages and relate them to whomever you meet." 8/16/1984

DEDICATION

It gives me great joy to dedicate this book to my earthly mother, Andrea Morin. Her constant prayers have influenced this writing and the *To The World* music. It was by the grace of God that I was given the privilege of visiting Medjugorje with her. I am eternally thankful to God for allowing this miracle of grace to take place in both of our lives. My mother's words at Medjugorje, which initiated my mission, echoed the words of Mary at the Wedding Feast of Cana: *"Do whatever He tells you."*

It is with devotion and great love that I dedicate this book to my heavenly Mother, Mary, without whose influence this miracle would not have happened. It is to her Immaculate Heart that I consecrate *Medjugorje - Our Lady Speaks To The World.* I pray that all of God's intentions for the purpose of this book be fulfilled.

SPECIAL THANKS

My sincere heartfelt thanks to Regina Morin, Bill Kuhn, Frank Beard, Vicki Martin, Judy Ellsbury and Pat Lehr for their dedication and assistance in the editing of this book.

INVOCATION TO THE HOLY SPIRIT

Come Holy Spirit, Illuminator of the mind, heart and soul. We invoke you to bring forth Your light, making clear to all, the purpose for which we are called. Bring us the assurance and peace of knowing that we belong to You, Spirit of the Triune God, and make us susceptible to your promptings. Grant us the courage and love to act on Your behalf. Most Divine Advocate, Paraclete of Light, descend on us now making us mindful of Your most holy presence. Let Your gifts be manifested in and through us for the edification of Christ's Body, the Church. Amen. Come, Holy Spirit.

-Jerry Morin – received 4/12/1989 Medjugorje

PREFACE

Although this book has been inspired by the Blessed Lady's messages at Medjugorje, it is important to understand that the theme of these messages has been, and continues to be, conveyed by her throughout the world. Her words echo the Gospel message brought to us over 2000 years ago by her Son, Jesus, and the apostles. Three of the most famous supernatural apparitions of Mary, approved by the Church, include Guadalupe, Mexico in 1531 where she appeared to Blessed Juan Diego and ultimately left her imprint on the renowned Tilma; Lourdes, France in 1864, where the Virgin Mary identified herself to young Bernadette Soubirous as the "Immaculate Conception"; then in 1917 at Fatima, Portugal to three young children, Lucia Dos Santos, Jacinta and Francisco Marto, where she revealed herself as the "Lady of the Rosary." Much of the public, however, are not aware of the numerous other Marian apparitions, many of which have been approved by the Church and many more under study and discernment.

With more frequency than ever before, it appears that the Mother of God is impressing throughout the world that prayer, fasting, penance, conversion and faith are essential to the peace and survival of this world. The performance of these acts, the Blessed Lady tells us, will lead us on the path to peace, great joy, and personal salvation.

In the 20th century alone there were over 500 reported visits of Mary to this planet. 386 cases have been studied by the Church. Of the 386 cases only 8 have met the criteria of the rigorous discernment process of the Church as being of supernatural character. The remaining majority of the cases are still in the process of discernment and a decision has not been reached. (1)

On every continent and in nearly every region of the globe Mary's presence has been experienced. In the approved Zeitun, Egypt transfiguration apparitions beginning in 1968, an estimated 250,000 people of all walks of life and all faiths saw an astounding vision of light above the St Mary's Coptic Orthodox Church for hours at a time. I believe this incredible display of Mary is more relevant today than even then. The Zeitun apparitions lasted for over two years in silence. The images of Mary were various and clearly visible. Her many historical depictions were seen in an unknown phosphorous type light during the apparitions. Luminous dovelike supernatural creatures also accompanied her. This event was approved by the Catholic Church and the Coptic Orthodox Church. It is documented that over one million people witnessed the apparitions. Our Lady would be clearly visible for as many as eight hours at a time.

Jesus spoke about the importance of discerning the signs of the times. In Mathew chapter 16, Jesus said, *"A wicked and adulterous generation looks for a miraculous sign, but none will be given it except the sign of Jonah."* In looking at the Book of Jonah we see that he was used by God to convey the message of impending destruction to the sin-laden city of Nineveh. Immediately the Ninevites began intense prayer and fasting. *"When God saw what they did and how they turned from their evil ways, he had compassion and did not bring upon them the destruction He had threatened."* (Jonah 3:10)

What better sign for discernment could the Lord send than that of His own Mother, warning and pleading for all of her children to be reconciled, purified and made whole? There is no doubt in Medjugorje, by the content of the messages, that God has a great concern for mankind. As history unfolds it is apparent that more and more people are closely watching Medjugorje. The seriousness of her messages leave no doubt that mankind could be reaching a critical time in history. In her messages, similarly conveyed in many apparition sites throughout history, she urges man to turn from sin and assures us that God does respond to prayer, fasting and repentance. The Blessed Lady reminds the visionaries of

Medjugorje that prayer and penitential acts can mitigate impending chastisements and even stop wars. Should we live in fear of what God holds for the future of this world? No! Rather, our energies should be spent centering prayer around the hope that the world will respond to the Blessed Lady's appeal for conversion, as the city of Nineveh did to Jonah's warning of old.

Chapter 1
Medjugorje

The small village of Medjugorje is located in the southwestern region of Bosnia and Herzegovina, country on the Balkan Peninsula, Southeastern Europe. The Balkan Peninsula is located between the Adriatic and Black Sea. It is here where simple, hardworking people tend their sheep and cultivate their grape orchards and tobacco farms. They also spend much time cultivating their faith, for here there is a strong devotion to God. The thirteen-ton cross at the top of the mountain called Krizevac is physical evidence of this deeply rooted spirituality. The Christian faith, dating back to the seventh century has been tested through time by the elements of centuries old warring factions and repressive communist influences. The Franciscans, as missionaries in the fourteenth century in the face of martyrdom, strengthened and preserved the Christian faith and have provided a strong influence for the entire region ever since. Much Franciscan blood has been shed in sacrifice for the Faith in this region over many centuries.

On June 24, 1981, the Catholic Feast of St. John the Baptist, two young women claimed to have seen a vision of a beautiful lady who later described herself as the Blessed Virgin Mary. The vision was first encountered while casually walking along the base of the hill Podbrdo, close to the village of Bijakovici in the parish of Medjugorje. The beautiful lady appeared for 45 minutes. The next day, on returning with others, they again experienced the vision. This was the beginning of the reported visions to two young women, along with four other friends, that have continued for over 30 years. These six visionaries have experienced a privilege granted to only a few select individuals in Christian history – a visual encounter with the Mother of Jesus. The names of the visionaries Vicka Ivankovic, Marija Pavlovic, Ivan Dragicevic, Jakov Colo, Mirjana Dragicevic and Ivanka Ivankovic are mentioned here with a full update on their status at the end of this book. Marija, Ivan and Mirjana, who are now in in the prime of life, still communicate with the Mother of God on a regular basis. As of the date of this publication, the Church is formally studying the events.

The ages of the visionaries at the onset of the apparitions ranged from ten to seventeen years of age. All were tested extensively and were found to be normal, healthy individuals. The beautiful lady revealed her reason for coming to this mountain village.

I come to tell you God exists. He is Truth. True happiness and the fullness of life are in Him. From another early message: *I have come because there are many good believers. I want to be with you, to convert and reconcile everyone.* She urged: *Peace, Peace, only peace. Reconcile yourselves. Peace must take place between God and man and between men.*

To date over 35,000 messages have been delivered through the visionaries to the world. People continue to visit Medjugorje from all parts of the world. Many of the early messages clearly accentuate her reason and purpose for appearing. The intensity and duration of the apparitions, enduring for over 30 years, is a testament to God's love for mankind. Although many are aware of these events, still the majority of mankind is unaware.

At one point Mary revealed to the seers: *I cannot heal..... Only God can. I need your prayers and sacrifices to help me.* On another occasion, she said: *Please pray to Jesus. I am His Mother and I intercede for you with Him, but all prayer goes to Jesus. I will help, I will pray, but everything does not depend only on me. It depends also on your strength and the strength of those who pray.* These very words support how the Church and countless millions have honored Mary as intercessor to Jesus on behalf of mankind.

From the context of Our Lady's early messages given to the seers, it appears her mission is that of one who has been sent by God. Through grace she is being allowed to bring messages not only to the visionaries, but to the local parish of Medjugorje and TO THE WORLD.

As a matter of comparison, the apparitions of Fatima, Portugal in 1917 involved the aspect of visible supernatural phenomena and secrets given to the three seers. In Medjugorje the Mother of Jesus confides ten secrets to the seers and many physical manifestations have been reported and witnessed. Some of these secrets are to be associated with visible signs and to-be-announced world events. The secrets are to be proof that the apparitions at Medjugorje are real and that the conversion back to God must be taken seriously. When the apparitions cease, Our Lady promised a visible, permanent sign left on the hill where she first appeared. Mirjana, one of the visionaries, has been quoted to say: "After the first warning, the others will follow within a brief period of time. So it is that people will have time for conversion. This time is a period of grace and conversion. After the visible sign, those who are still alive will have little time for conversion. For that reason the Blessed Virgin calls for urgent conversion and reconciliation." The Blessed Lady also mentioned that the seventh secret, which was a serious matter, was negated due to the fasting and prayers of many believers. She further stated that the ninth and tenth secrets are grave matters and are chastisements for the sins of the world. These, she says, cannot be changed, but they can be lessened with prayer and fasting.

The message of the visible sign is best expressed by the Blessed Mother's own words: *This sign will be given for the unbelievers. You faithful, already have signs, and you yourselves must become the signs for the unbelievers… You, faithful, must not wait for the sign before you convert.*

Convert soon, for this time is a time of grace for you. This time is for deepening your faith and your conversion. When the sign comes, it will be too late for many. She respects and is aware that each person has free will and the power to choose. However, she persistently asks, and at times seems to beg, for prayer and our commitment to **LIVE THE MESSAGES** she conveys.

At the same time as the onset of the apparitions at Medjugorje, the Church approved supernatural events at Kibeho (Rwanda, Africa) were taking place. The apparitions of Our Lady of Kibeho began on November 28, 1981. She appeared at a time of great distress in the region as the "Mother of The Word." She correctly prophesied the Rwandan Genocide of 1994.

Since June of 1981, the frequency of the messages in Medjugorje has gone through successive stages of delivery. In the beginning, Our Lady of Medjugorje conveyed a message nearly every night. After a few years, although visits were daily, her messages decreased to once a week. The messages then evolved to being conveyed on the 25th day of each month and continue to the date of this publication.

The visionaries report they see her as a three dimensional figure and, much like the visionaries of other apparition sites, describe her as the most beautiful woman ever seen. Bernadette Soubirous, in her encounter with the Lady at Lourdes, France in 1864, described the Lady as exceedingly beautiful as did the two young visionaries at LaSalette, France in 1846.In Medjugorje, as in many of her visits throughout history, Mary appears standing above the ground on a cloud in a very bright light and identifies herself as "The Queen of Peace". The visionaries say they see a diadem of 12 stars around her head as is described in the 12th chapter of Revelation. When they are experiencing this mystery, they are completely enraptured. To the observer, they appear to be in a completely different state of existence, as though transcended in time and space.

Referenced earlier are Mary's titles at Lourdes and Fatima. In LaSalette, France in 1846 she portrayed herself as "The Lady of Sorrows". At Pontmaine, France in 1871, she appeared as "The Lady of Hope". In 1932 she appeared at Beauraing, Belgium and was quoted as saying, "*I will convert sinners.*" At Banneaux, France, 1933, she was perceived as "The Virgin of the Poor". In 1968 in the church approved apparitions of Zeitun, Egypt, she appeared to thousands at a time and seen above the dome of the St. Mary's Coptic Orthodox Church. At Zeitun she has the title of "Our Lady of Light". The apparition was total silence. There she was viewed by the multitudes for up to eight hours at a time for over two years. In another church approved apparition site in Venezuela, South America, beginning in 1976 she appeared to visionary Maria Esperanza. There she appeared as "Reconciler of People and Nations".

Throughout all these appearances our Blessed Lady has consistently conveyed clear and loving messages divinely reflecting God's patience in dealing with humanity.

The last thirty plus years have yielded a great deal of research and writings concerning the apparitions at Medjugorje. I would encourage not only further reading of these present day apparitions, but further study of earlier documented Marian apparitions throughout Christian history. My own research has led me to a solid conclusion. This marvelous Lady has had, and continues to have, a great impact on God's Plan of Salvation for the world by gently leading many toward a deeper understanding of her Son, Jesus. To many, she is a clear reflection of God's tender mercy and grace.

The messages of prayer, fasting, faith and conversion are central to Medjugorje and to the Gospel. She asks us to live these messages daily, and by living them, true peace will abide. And when each of us reaches out for this peace, then that peace will prevail. Medjugorje is truly a Christocentric message TO THE WORLD.

After my second trip to Medjugorje in April, 1989, I was inspired to write a meditative handbook designed to correlate the Blessed Lady's messages with accompanying Scripture passages. It is a spiritual supplement to the *To The World* music, given to me on my initial visit to this grace-filled place. The original meditative handbook is incorporated into this book and re-published as <u>*Medjugorje Our Lady Speaks To The World.*</u> I pray that it serves as a "fruit" and witness of the conversion power through Our Lady at Medjugorje.

In retrospect, Scripture has had a deep impact on my life through the years, and it was Scripture that confirmed my mysterious leading to Medjugorje. A careful analysis of her messages, in relation to embedded Holy Scripture within my mind and heart, led to a tremendous respect and love for how the Blessed Lady is being used as God's instrument for peace and salvation. Because my life has been rooted in Scripture for many years, it was to be these confirmations of "The Word" that led me to the events and message of Medjugorje. This belief of the Blessed Lady as God's instrument of peace and a prophet for this world has brought me to a deeper understanding of her role in salvation history. This awareness came from a very personal, internal assimilation and personal illumination which I can only attribute to the **Holy Spirit** of God. This illumination and awareness has also subsequently created a deeper awareness of her influence on bringing me closer to her Son, Jesus.

Because of my earlier search for truth, I had the fortune of experiencing many varieties of worship with the Christian framework. Because Scripture is central to our Christian faith, the messages of the Blessed Lady accentuate her requests of peace, prayer, fasting, faith and conversion and are presented in this book with accompanying Scripture for reflection and meditation. (The reader may also listen to many of the messages on the audio CD: *Queen of Peace Messages To The World.*)

It is my hope that for those who do not read Scripture regularly, this book will encourage further reading, resulting in a deeper understanding of Mary and her role in Medjugorje, in the Christian Faith and in the world, leading to a more personal relationship with Jesus, the Lord, and His Gospel message. Our Lady is here for **all people:** her messages are universally filled with a motherly love and concern for the salvation of all people.

It is also my hope that Christians who have not experienced the gentle integration of the Blessed Lady into their faith, and therefore have not experienced the wonderful graces which the Holy Spirit presents through her, will be illuminated with a fresh view and more open heart towards her. Then, in light of Holy Scripture, all will see more clearly God's Mother as His special instrument of peace in this troubled world.

1Timothy 2:5 confirms that Jesus is the one true mediator between God and man. However, by grace, it is being clearly shown to many that Mary is a beautiful Mediatrix between Jesus and man. She is special beyond the mere belief of an ordinary woman. This chosen woman brought the Christ into this world initially and continues to re-present Him, through the Spirit, to the world over and over again. Every Marian apparition is for the purpose of re-presenting Him to the world and serves as a reminder of what Jesus teaches us. She comes to remind us of how our lives should be lived.

God's graces through this magnificent Lady are a great mystery and are available to anyone who accepts her as their Heavenly Mother - the Mother of our Christian faith. This very special woman, and her spouse the Holy Spirit, procreated the greatest gift known to mankind. There is no woman like this mother. She is the first Christian, the first one to say "yes" to Christ, the first tabernacle, the first Apostle, the perfect model of surrender to God's calling in our own life. "*May it be done to me according to your word*." (Luke 1:38). Her concern extends beyond all denominational and cultural differences. Her call goes out to people of all nations. She wants all to be considered her children. She, in turn, asks us to have the faith of a child in surrendering our lives into God's hands. Jesus said. *"Amen, I say to you, unless you turn and become like children, you will not enter the kingdom of heaven."*(Matthew18:3) It is interesting to note that most of her appearances have been to young children. She will lovingly take any one to her Son's cross where reconciliation and conversion begin. Increased faith and peace is what she promises to those who follow her model of surrender to God.

In a world with potential for complete self-destruction, it's no wonder God would send His Mother. I find it no coincidence that her appearances in Medjugorje began on the Catholic Church feast day of St. John the Baptist. If one is attentive to her messages, one can almost hear the same prophetic spirit of this great saint quoting Isaiah, *"I am the voice of one calling in the desert. 'Make straight the way for the Lord."* John the Baptist called for repentance in proclaiming the Messiah. The similarity exists in that Mary's call stresses repentance and conversion. In Medjugorje Mary said that these will be her last appearances in our times. Is she the prophet heralding Jesus the Lord? Is she preparing the spiritual crib of the world? It certainly seems she is preparing the way for an incredible time. Be it His return, be it chastisements or be it warning, shouldn't we be fully prepared always?

Most of the world did not listen to Christ over 2000 years ago. Should we be surprised if the world does not listen today? Each of us who has been called by grace to salvation has a unique responsibility in living the Gospel message of Christ and the message of Medjugorje in faith. Drawing closer to Christ and to God eliminates any fear of His plan for this world. By walking the path of salvation we become noticeably less conformed to the ways of the world as we become transcended in faith toward heavenly matters. Building up "treasures" for the Kingdom becomes a priority. Each of us continues, hand in hand, in the walk toward our heavenly home, one hand in the Blessed Lady's and the other in Jesus. Mary's call is a personal call to every soul and it requires a response of personal responsibility toward one's own salvation.

Although her messages are delivered with a gentle and peaceful tone, the sense of urgency is unmistakable. I pray that the reader is blessed with his own experiential witness in knowing the wonderful graces of God through the Blessed Lady. Scripture tells us that by grace through faith we are saved. I have never experienced more grace than the Holy Spirit's manifestations through this extraordinary woman, who brings me so gently into the Throne Room of Grace. Hail Mary! Full of grace.

The following Marian messages, Scriptural verses and reflections are offered in the spirit of love. May the peace of Jesus and the influence of this Heavenly Mother, "Queen of Peace", be with us all in our journey homeward.

"Therefore, if anyone is in Christ, he is a new creation; the old has gone, the new has come! All this is from God, who has reconciled us to Himself through Christ and gave us the ministry of reconciliation: that God was reconciling the world to himself in Christ, not counting men's sins against them. And he has committed to us the message of reconciliation. We are therefore Christ's ambassadors, as though God were making his appeal through us. We implore you on Christ's behalf: Be reconciled to God. God made him who had no sin to be sin for us, so that in him we might become the righteousness of God."

(2 Corinthians 5:17-21)

Chapter 2
Medjugorje Our Lady Speaks To The World Live the Message

PRAYER, FAITH, FASTING, CONVERSION AND PEACE

To live the message is the request and the directive that the Blessed Virgin Mary is exhorting to the world in Medjugorje. The message is essentially the same that her Son, Jesus, gave to the world over 2,000 years ago: by faith in prayer and through repentance we can come to know and experience the joy of living with the Spirit that God promised to us. His Spirit, the Spirit of Truth, would be with us and would dwell in us, testifying to us within our own mind, heart and soul of His truth. Jesus said: ***"Amen, amen, I say to you, no one can enter the Kingdom of God without being born of water and Spirit. What is born of flesh is flesh and what is born of spirit is spirit."*** (John 2:5-6). People are quickly finding out that true lasting joy does not stem from the flesh or the materialism of this world. So many people are restless and bored, finding no real purpose and direction in life. Through the Blessed Virgin in Medjugorje, God is urging us to find Him, and thus peace now!

HOLY SPIRIT (KEY UNDERSTANDING)

I wish to take a moment to express a personal insight that I believe God granted to me through an infusion of His grace. I mentioned earlier that it was Scripture that profoundly confirmed to me the presence of Mary in Medjugorje and throughout the world. I wish to try to assist the reader in comprehending the incomprehensible. Jesus declared to His apostles that His Father would be sending a promised gift of Holy Spirit. Look at these important words. Jesus said: ***"I will ask the Father and he will give you another Advocate to be with you always, the Spirit of truth which the world cannot accept because it neither sees nor knows him*** (John 14:16-17). These are the words of Jesus describing the Third Person of the Holy Trinity. Our Lady said in one of her first messages, *"I come to tell you God exists,* **He is Truth.** *True happiness and the fullness of life are in Him."* When you begin to make these kinds of connections over and over again, the hair begins to stand up straight on your arms. Here is another example ***"But the Helper, the Holy Spirit, whom the Father will send in My name, He will teach you all things, and bring to your remembrance all that I said to you."*** (John 14:26)

Remember, Mary was the instrument overshadowed with the Holy Spirit to cooperate in a virgin birth. In an incomprehensible act through a supernatural entity, Mary became part of the Supernatural from that point to today. In Lourdes, France, The Virgin Mother said *"I am the Immaculate Conception."* Her supernatural participation with God even begins at her own birth.

As a writer and composer of lyrics and music I have cultivated an awareness and great appreciation that this Holy Spirit is very active and operative if one allows it. Marvelous insights and illuminations of truth can be received if one will let it. I have learned it is all a matter of surrender to the Trinity: Father, Son and Holy Spirit. There are many references of Jesus in Scripture granting us the keys to communicate with God and His Holy Spirit. This can be better described as the channel of FAITH. This is why so many are very attentive and obedient to the messages of Our Lady.

I believe God sends His Mother to bear witness to the **truth**, **reminding** us of the urgency to return to, remain in, or find new the Truth which is spoken by her Son. ***"For God*** *so loved the world that He gave His only begotten Son, so that everyone who believes in Him might not perish, but have eternal life. God did not send His Son into the world to condemn the world, but that the world might be saved through Him"* (John 3:16-17).

Keep in mind that the bottom line in all of this is our eternal existence. That illumination also can be brought to you through the Spirit of Truth.

Prayer, fasting, faith, conversion and peace are all essential keys that the Blessed Lady so patiently explains are necessary for our salvation. She wants these keys exercised and all of her children centered on Jesus and God in total trust. This trust is exhorted as a "surrender" totally to God, a surrender that is trusting like a little child. To be "saved" is the desire she wishes for all her children. She respectfully recommends for us to make the **choice** of surrendering to God. God knows the urgency of the times and He hopes that we grasp the importance of listening to His Mother.

PRAYER

This is the Blessed Lady's most requested message. It is through prayer that all communication with God begins. The Blessed Lady continually asks us to *"pray, pray, pray."* She asks us to pray from the heart. It is important that the heart be cleansed and purified. In this way our prayer from the heart can be sent through the open channel to God unobstructed. She stresses personal confession as a means of truly purifying the heart. For Catholics, she asks for frequent confessions, at least monthly, for great graces flow through the act of personal confession. It is each individual's personal responsibility to prepare and cleanse his or her own heart. Then our channel is open to God and the personal two-way communication can begin. On August 25, 1989 the Blessed Lady says," *Dear children, I call you to prayer. By means of prayer little children, you obtain joy and peace. Through prayer, you are richer in the mercy of God. Therefore, little children, let your prayer be the life for each one of you. Especially, I call you to pray so that all of them that are far away from God may be converted. Then all hearts shall be richer because God will rule in the hearts of all men. I thank you for your response to my call."*

The Blessed Lady at another time said that if we knew the result of prayer we would want to pray constantly.

There are many forms of prayer. We should always ask Our Lord and the Holy Spirit to guide us in our methods of prayer. The Our Father was the spiritual prayer taught by Jesus. The Blessed Lady at Medjugorje has revealed that **"The Rosary"** is the prayer now that Satan hates the most. And yes, her messages reveal she has an enemy. She clearly mentions it as Satan. We need to believe in the power of this scriptural prayer now more than ever before. Today the world offers TV programming of such things as house haunting, search of ghosts, alien astronaut theories, and paranormal shows of all kinds. People are tremendously enamored with the supernatural and would like to try to make sense of what this existence is all about. The Lady at Medjugorje reveals many spiritual illuminations. I don't see where any of these other offerings offer the viewer the keys for their eternal happiness. Mary does! The late Pope John Paul II actually encouraged people to visit Medjugorje. One very predominant message from the now Blessed John Paul II is, **"Today the world has lost its sense of the supernatural, but many are searching for it - and find it in Medjugorje through prayer, fasting and penance."** If you've never prayed a **rosary** before….start now! In the fourth apparition of Fatima, Our Lady identified herself as "The Lady of the Rosary". She told the children: *"Pray, pray a great deal and make sacrifices for sinners, for many souls go to Hell for not having someone to pray and make sacrifices for them."* On September 6, 1984 in a message at Medjugorje she said: *"Dear children, there is no peace without prayer. So I tell*

you, dear children, to pray for peace in front of the cross."
Our Lady at Fatima prophesied the end of World War I and the greater World War II in which over 60 million people perished. In Medjugorje she has imparted secrets to the visionaries. Many of the secrets are associated with events she prophecies will take place as a result of the sins of mankind.

One of the great vehicles to prayer is the Holy Bible. The Blessed Lady at Medjugorje requests for us to **read it regularly**. I was very enthused when I had discovered that Mary herself was encouraging the reading of Holy Scripture. She asks us to have it in a prominent place in the home so that we can be reminded to read it often. Saint Augustine once said: "When you pray you talk to God. When you read the Holy Bible God talks to you." Prayer brings a clarity and an illumination to discernment which we desperately need in discerning good from evil. The Virgin Mary tells us to pray to receive the Holy Spirit, for with the **Holy Spirit** you have everything. To the locutionist Jelena in Medjugorje, Our Lady revealed:

*"I'm going to reveal a **spiritual secret** to you: if you want to be stronger than evil, make yourself a plan of personal prayer Take a certain time in the morning, read a text from Holy Scripture, anchor the Divine word in your heart, and strive to live it during the day, particularly during the moment of trials. In this way, you will be stronger than evil."*

FAITH

In prayer we take the time and opportunity to thank and praise God in gratitude for the graces and blessings He has bestowed. We bring our petitions and our needs in prayer. Then, when God answers our petitions and supplications, faith is increased. We begin to experience a God that cares for us personally. This faith to believe, even though we have not yet seen the answer, is the kind of faith God desires. Our Lady echoed this herself in one of her earliest messages. ***"Blessed are they who have not seen and yet still believe"*** (John 20:29). Mary again becomes a wonderful example during the wedding feast at Cana when she instructed the servants to ***"do whatever He tells you."***(John2:5) It is to this kind of faith that Mary is calling us. She urges us to trust totally in God for our answers and direction in life… to do whatever we hear Him tell us to do, whether through Scripture or direct personal revelation. This kind of faith takes courage, but the way to peace is achieved by being in the Will of God. He knows far greater than us what we need for complete fulfillment and wholeness in this life.

This total trust, total surrender, is the core of our Christian faith. The more we surrender and trust in God and in the Son, Jesus Christ, the more we experience God at work in our lives. When we begin to taste the results of surrender to God, faith increases. Increased works of the heart are manifested. We become led from one glory to another. Our lives then begin to bear fruit.

Faith in Jesus Christ is what is asked in Scripture and what Our Blessed Lady desires of us. Increased faith leads us to a desire to proclaim His name and to <u>give witness to the world of what He is doing with our lives.</u> We become a light for others to see. Jesus said, ***"Therefore whoever confesses Me before men, him I will also confess before My Father who is in heaven"*** (Matthew 10:32). About faith He said; ***"Verily I say unto you, If ye have faith and doubt not ye shall not only do this which is done to the fig tree, but also if ye say to this mountain, be thou removed…it shall be done"*** (Matthew 21:21). Paul tells us, ***"but without faith it is impossible to please Him, for he that cometh to God must believe that He is, and that He is a rewarder of them that diligently seek Him"*** (Hebrews 11:6).

Faith and trust in Jesus Christ loosens and breaks the bondage of sin in our lives. The apostle Paul tells us that it's not a flesh and blood fight, but the unseen battle of principalities. For this reason it is imperative that we have the greatest spiritual Principality with us, Jesus the Christ. He broke the hold and bondage of sin through His death on the cross. If we could grasp the importance of His death to our everyday lives we would be invoking His Spirit continually. We would also experience far fewer troubles. By His death and resurrection he became the victor over Satan and all his evil works. What peace there is in knowing that we have the ultimate conqueror on our side. The Virgin Mary also has been revealed to be granted great power over her adversary, Satan. Genesis 3:15 indicates the battle that she would be engaged in. Chapter 12 describes the way the seers have described Mary *"A great and wondrous sign appeared in heaven: a woman clothed with the sun, with the moon under her feet and a crown of twelve stars on her head."* That same chapter describes how Satan went on to wage war with the rest of her offspring. Who are the rest of her offspring? In the next sentence that question is answered: *"...those who keep the commandments and give witness to Jesus Christ"* (Rev 12:17).

FASTING

The act of fasting on a regular basis is foreign to most of us. It became a revelation to many when our Mary emphasized not only prayer but fasting as well. We have learned much in this school of Mary. She calls to fast two days a week on bread and water. It is an act of self-denial and serves to remind us of God on those days. Mary has revealed incredible insight as to the power and relevance of prayer and fasting together. Many were illuminated to the power in her words when she stated that prayer and fasting can prevent and stop wars, can even change the laws of nature. Her words bring hope, in that no matter how difficult things seem to appear, that we can make a difference through prayer and fasting. In one of her early messages, when first illuminating the world to Medjugorje's connection to Fatima she said: *"Dear Children! Today also I invite you to prayer, now as never before when my plan has begun to be realized. Satan is strong and wants to sweep away plans of peace and joy and make you think that my Son is not strong in his decisions. Therefore, I call all of you, dear children to **pray and fast still more firmly**. I invite you to realize through the secrets I began in Fatima may be fulfilled. I call you, dear children, to grasp the importance of my coming and the seriousness of the situation. I want to save all souls and present them to God. Therefore, let us pray that everything I have begun be fully realized. Thank you for having responded to my call."*

The concept of fasting is not new. Its proof of effectiveness is found throughout the Old and New Testaments. It is a regular part of many religious customs in the world. It is a form of spiritual discipline to elevate our spiritual consciousness. It increases clarity and adds to discernment. Christian and non-Christian religions throughout history maintain fasting. This form of spiritual discipline is again one of the key requests that she asks of us.

Christ referred to fasting as an effective prerequisite when He told His apostles that there were some evil spiritual possessions that would only be removed by prayer and fasting.

Remember it was through prayer and fasting that the Ninevites heeded and responded to the warning of Jonah of God's impending destruction. They took the warning seriously and responded. Will we do the same now?

In a message on September 25, 1985 she said: *"Dear children, thank you for all your prayers. Thank you for all your sacrifices. I want to renew the messages that I am giving you. **Heed the call to fasting** because by fasting you* *will ensure the total plan of God here in Medjugorje will be fulfilled. That will give me great joy."*

Jesus said, **"But when you fast, put oil on your head and wash your face, so that it will not be obvious to men that you are fasting, but only to your Father, who is unseen; and your Father, who sees what is done is secret will reward you"** (Matthew 6:17-18).

CONVERSION

The following is a portion of the Blessed Virgin's message of January 25, 1988: *"Dear children, today again I am calling you to complete conversion, which is difficult for those who have not chosen God. I am inviting you, dear children, to convert fully to God."*

Webster's dictionary defines "convert" as to bring over from one belief, view, or party to another. The conversion experience can be as powerful and dramatic as the apostle Paul's conversion on his way to Damascus, or it can be a subtle, gradual change such as is happening to many at Medjugorje. Conversion itself is a function of God's grace, God's timing and our willingness to be open to Him. Recall that St. Augustine's mother, St. Monica, prayed for his conversion all her life. It was not until the end of her life that she witnessed her prayers answered. Not only was Augustine converted from a life of sin and self-indulgence, but miraculously went on to be declared "Doctor of the Church."

The Blessed Lady is calling us to complete conversion. This can only be accomplished through complete surrender – surrender to God and **His Spirit**.

Jesus tells us in Scripture that we must be converted and be like little children in order to enter the kingdom of heaven.

To develop the trusting heart of a child, we must voluntarily turn from evil and choose God every day. The power of individual choice is respected by the Blessed Lady and God, but the wrong choice can lead to spiritual and eternal death. Our goal is eternal life. Romans 12:2 says ***"And be not conformed to this world; but be ye transformed by the renewing of your mind; that ye may prove what is good, and acceptable, and perfect will of God."***

The path to conversion means trusting in Jesus Christ. Our Lady brings us to Him and He makes the changes if we are willing to allow Him to be the Lord of our lives. Surrender can be a joy when we realize that God truly wants us to be happy and that He knows what is best for us.

Conversion is essential to salvation and today God is sending His Mother as a divine catalyst for conversion TO THE WORLD.

We have watched what appears to be an onslaught on the Catholic Church and on the Christian faith in general. Our Late Blessed Pope John Paul II had been reported to speak of Medjugorje as a "continuation of Fatima." The Church will be the final judge of Medjugorje, and whatever the outcome, nothing can change the fact that my life has joined countless others in becoming a witness to conversion, that mystical change of heart with its infusions of grace coming through Our Lady of Medjugorje.

PEACE

On October 29, 1983, the Lady of Medjugorje said: *"Prayer is the only way that leads to peace. If you pray and fast, you will obtain all you ask."*

In another message given November 29, 1983 Mary said: *"I am your good Mother, but Jesus is your great friend. Fear nothing in His presence, but give Him your hearts. From the depth of your heart tell Him your sufferings, In this way you will be revitalized in prayer, your heart set free, and in peace, without fear."*

Peace is a by-product of prayer. The Virgin Mary desires us to be in a continuous prayerful state of mind. Prayer increases faith and peace. Mary comes to Medjugorje as the "Queen of Peace." Like Fatima, peace is her desire. The Blessed Mother urges us to receive the peace of God, now, during this special time of outpouring of God's great graces. We then can face the uncertain future with internal peace and without fear, a peace that only God can give, a peace that this world does not offer. Jesus said: **"*I have told you these things, so that in me you may have peace. In this world you will have trouble. But take heart! I have overcome the world"*** (John 16:33).

June 5, 1986

*"Dear children, today I am calling you to decide whether or not you want to **live my messages.** I am calling you to become active in **living and carrying my messages to others**. I desire that all of you become the living image of Jesus and bear witness to this unfaithful world. I desire that you become a light to all and that you witness to everyone around you. Dear children, you are not called to darkness; you are called to become a light. **So be a light by the way you give witness with your lives**. Thank you for responding to my call."*

Blessed Virgin Mary at Medjugorje

Love your neighbor as yourself. Love does not harm its neighbor. Therefore love is the fulfillment of the law. And do this, understanding the present time. The hour has come for you to wake up from your slumber, because our salvation is nearer now that when we first believed. The night is nearly over; the day is almost here. So let us put aside the deeds of darkness and put on the armor of light... clothe yourselves with the Lord Jesus Christ, and do not think of the sinful nature.

(Romans 13:9-14)

Chapter 3
Medjugorje Our Lady Speaks To The World

Message, Scripture, Reflection

January 8, 1987

Dear children! I want to thank you for your response to my messages; especially dear children thank you for all the sacrifices and prayers you have presented to me. I want to continue, dear children, to give you messages, no longer every Thursday, but on the 25th of each month. The time has come when all that my Lord wanted has been fulfilled. From now on I will give you fewer messages but I will still be with you. Dear children, I ask you to listen to my messages and to live them so that I can guide you. Thank you for responding to my call.

You were shown these things so that you might know that the LORD is God; besides him there is no other. From heaven he made you hear his voice to discipline you. On earth he showed you his great fire, and you heard his words from out of the fire. (Deuteronomy 4:35-36)

Reflection: Lord, out of the heavens You send Your Mother to instruct and guide us. Your Mother is here on Your behalf. Help me to take these words of wisdom and direction seriously, and to listen intently as my faith reaffirms Your messages delivered through this marvelous Lady.

January 25, 1987

Dear children! Today I want to appeal to all of you to start living a new life from this day forward. I want you to understand that God has chosen each one of you to have a part in His great plan for the salvation of mankind. You cannot grasp fully how great your role is in God's plan. For this reason, dear children, pray so that through prayer you may penetrate more deeply into an understanding of God's design for you. I am with you so that you can fulfill it completely. Thank you for responding to my call.

For this is what the Lord has commanded us: " 'I have made you a light for the Gentiles, that you may bring salvation to the ends of the earth.'" (Acts 13:47)

Reflection: Lord, I believe there are no coincidences when walking on the path to salvation. Help me to understand that time is important, and that my life does make a difference in Your Divine Plan. I give you the room You need to fulfill completely that which You began in me. I have decided not to let my light be hidden under a bushel basket, but to let it shine for all to see.

February 25, 1987

Dear children! Today I want to wrap you all in my mantle and lead you all along the way of conversion. Dear children, I beseech you, surrender to the Lord your entire past, all the evil that has accumulated in your hearts. I want each one of you to be happy, but in sin nobody can be happy. Therefore, dear children, pray, and in prayer you shall realize a new way of joy. Joy will manifest in your hearts and thus you shall be joyful witnesses of that which I and My Son want from each one of you. I am blessing you. Thank you for having responded to my call.

Peter replied, "Repent and be baptized, every one of you, in the name of Jesus Christ for the forgiveness of your sins. And you will receive the gift of the Holy Spirit. The promise is for you and your children and for all who are far off--for all whom the Lord our God will call."
(Acts 2:38-39)

Reflection: Lord, through my personal confession, You promise to remove my sins as far from me as the east is from the west. Come, Holy Spirit, as you came to the Upper Room to Mary and the apostles and let me join in the same joy they experienced.

March 25, 1987

*Dear children! Today I am grateful to you for your presence in this place, where I am giving you special graces. I call each one of you to begin to live as of today that life which God wishes of you and to begin to perform good works of love and mercy. I do not want you, dear children, to **live the message** and be committing sin which is displeasing to me. Therefore, dear children, I want each of you to live a new life without destroying all that God produces in you and is giving you. I give you my special blessing and I am remaining with you on your way of conversion. Thank you for having responded to my call.*

As a prisoner for the Lord, then, I urge you to live a life worthy of the calling you have received. Be completely humble and gentle; be patient, bearing with one another in love. Make every effort to keep the unity of the Spirit through the bond of peace. There is one body and one Spirit--just as you were called to one hope when you were called -- one Lord one faith, one baptism; one God and Father of all who is over all and through all and in all. (Ephesians 4:1-6)

Reflection: Father, my awareness of new life is reaffirmed by Your Mother. I accept You, Jesus, in my heart as Lord and Savior as Your Mother would wish. I make You the center of my life. I make You first in my life, for You know far greater than I what is best for my life. In all happenings I surrender to You.

April 25, 1987

Dear children! Today also I am calling you to prayer. You know, dear children, that God grants special graces in prayer. Therefore, seek and pray in order that you may be able to comprehend all that I am giving here. I call you, dear children, to prayer with the heart. You know that without prayer you cannot comprehend all that God is planning through each one of you. Therefore, pray! I desire that through each one of you God's plan may be fulfilled, that all which God has planted in your heart may keep on growing. So pray that God's blessing may protect each one of you from all the evil that is threatening you. I bless you, dear children. Thank you for having responded to my call.

And this is my prayer: that your love may abound more and more in knowledge and depth of insight, so that you may be able to discern what is best and may be pure and blameless until the day of Christ, filled with the fruit of righteousness that comes through Jesus Christ--to the glory and praise of God. (Philippians 1:9-11)

Reflection: Prayer, Blessed Lady, is what you emphasize. It's true that prayer enhances our abilities to discern what is best. It helps me to prepare for listening to what God might be trying to tell me today. Help me to increasingly experience the value and the joy of prayer.

May 25, 1987

*Dear children! I am calling every one of you to start living in God's love. Dear children, you are ready to commit sin, and to put yourselves in the hands of Satan without reflecting. I call on each one of you to consciously decide for God and against Satan. I am your Mother and, therefore, I want to lead you all to perfect holiness. I want each one of you to be happy here on earth and to be with me in Heaven. That is, dear children, **the purpose of my coming here** and it's my desire. Thank you for having responded to my call.*

My children, I am writing this to you so that you may not commit sin. But if anyone does sin, we have an Advocate with the Father, Jesus Christ the righteous one. He is expiation for our sins, and not for our sins only, but for those of the whole world.(John 2:1-2)

Reflection: Thank You, O God, for being patient with us mortals here on earth. I decide again today for You, God. In my human frailty, forgive me for the many mistakes I make when I separate myself from You. It is clearly by Your grace that I am loved so much. Thank You for sending Your Mother in these uncertain times to remind us of the importance of staying close to You.

June 25, 1987

Dear children! Today I thank you and I want to invite you all to God's peace. I want each one of you to experience in your heart that peace which God gives. I want to bless you all today. I am blessing you with God's blessing and I beseech you, dear children, to follow and to live my way. I love you, dear children, and so not even counting the number of times, I go on calling you and I thank you for all that you are doing for my intentions. I beg you, help me to present you to God and to save you. Thank you for having responded to my call.

And you, child, will be called prophet of the Most High, for you will go before the Lord to prepare His ways, to give His people knowledge of salvation through the forgiveness of their sins because of the tender mercy of our God, by which the daybreak from on high will visit us to shine on those who sit in darkness and death's shadow, to guide our feet into the path of peace.(Luke 1:76-79)

Reflection: O God, Thank You for sending Your Mother on the Feast of St. John the Baptist. Like John, You are preparing and showing the way for our personal salvation. Grant me the grace, O Lord, to take the salvation message seriously.

July 25, 1987

Dear children, I beseech you to take up the way of holiness beginning today. I love you and, therefore, I want you to be holy. I do not want Satan to block you on that way. Dear children, pray and accept all that God is offering you on a way which is bitter. But at the same time, God will reveal every sweetness to whomever begins to go on that way, and He will gladly answer every call of God. Do not attribute importance to petty things. Long for Heaven. Thank you for having responded to my call.

I put this in human terms because you are weak in your natural selves. Just as you used to offer the parts of your body in slavery to impurity and to ever-increasing wickedness, so now offer them in slavery to righteousness leading to holiness. (Romans 6:19)

Reflection: By surrendering, Blessed Lady, to God and to your Son, Jesus, the path to holiness is made easier. I find that through my surrendering God leads me. I need but listen and follow.

August 25, 1987

*Dear children!, Today also I am calling you all in order that each one of you decides to **live my messages.** God has permitted me also in this year, which the Church has dedicated to me, to be able to speak to you and to be able to spur you on to holiness. Dear children, seek from God the graces which He is giving you through me. I am ready to intercede with God for all that you seek so that your holiness may be complete. Therefore, dear children, do not forget to seek, because God has permitted me to obtain graces for you. Thank you for having responded to my call.*

My soul proclaims the greatness of the Lord; my spirit rejoices in God my savior. For he has looked upon His handmaid's lowliness; behold, from now on will all ages call me blessed. The Mighty One has done great things for me and Holy is His name. His mercy is from age to age to those who fear Him. (Luke 1:46-50)

Reflection: Blessed Lady is your name. Scripture reminds me that you will always be called Blessed and that God had done great things for you. You are the chosen woman whom God called for His special plan. Father, I see now, as never before, the marvelous way in which You are using Your Mother. It's exciting to be living in these days.

September 25, 1987

Dear children! Today also I want to call you all to prayer. Let prayer be your life. Dear children, dedicate your time only to Jesus and He will give you everything that you are seeking. He will reveal Himself to you in fullness. Dear children, Satan is strong and is waiting to test each one of you. Pray, and that way he will neither be able to injure you nor block you on the way of holiness. Dear children, through prayer grow all the more toward God from day to day. Thank you for having responded to my call.

Then He returned to His disciples and found them sleeping. "Could you men not keep watch with Me for one hour?" He asked Peter. "Watch and pray so that you will not fall into temptation. The spirit is willing, but the body is weak. (Matthew 26:40-41)

Reflection: Mary, like a loving mother, you take the time to instruct us as your children. Thank you for teaching us the importance of prayer. Today I will lift up your prayer, the "Rosary," that you have asked us to pray. I am reminded that this prayer is scriptural and I meditate on Christ's life through the Joyful, Sorrowful, Glorious and Luminous mysteries.

October 25, 1987

My dear children! Today I want to call all of you to decide for Paradise. The way is difficult for those who have not decided for God. Dear children, decide and believe that God is offering Himself to you in His fullness. You are invited and you need to answer the call of the Father, Who is calling you through me. Pray, because in prayer each one of you will be able to achieve complete love. I am blessing you and I desire to help you so that each one of you might be under my motherly mantle. Thank you for having responded to my call.

I cried out to Him with my mouth. His praise was on my tongue. If I had cherished sin in my heart, the Lord would not have listened; but God has surely listened and heard my voice in prayer. Praise be to God, who has not rejected my prayer or withheld His love from me!
(Psalm 66:17-20)

Reflection: Blessed Mother, I am noticing that your love brings a sense of protection. I accept your caring for me and I respond by letting you know that I wish to remain under the protection of your mantle. I believe I am safe there. Keep me in your mantle, dear Lady.

November 25, 1987

Dear children, Today also I call each one of you to decide to surrender again everything completely to me. Only that way will I be able to present each of you to God. Dear children, you know that I love you immeasurably and that I desire each of you for myself, but God has given to all a freedom which I lovingly respect and humbly submit to. I desire, dear children, that you help so that everything God has planned in this parish shall be realized. If you do not pray, you shall not be able to recognize my love and the plans which God has for this parish and for each individual. Pray that Satan does not entice you with his pride and deceptive strength. I am with you and I want you to believe me, that I love you. Thank you for having responded to my call.

In the same way, the Spirit helps us in our weakness. We do not know what we ought to pray, but the Spirit Himself intercedes for us with groans that words cannot express. And He who searches our hearts knows the mind of the Spirit, because the Spirit intercedes for the saints in accordance with God's Will. (Romans 8:26-27)

Reflection: You are so gracious, Blessed Mother. In accepting the fact that we all have a free will. It's very clear that you understand it is all up to me. Your understanding of my free will makes it all the easier to listen to what the Father is telling me. I pray to know His Will for my life.

December 25, 1987

Dear children! Rejoice with me! My heart is rejoicing because of Jesus and today I want to give Him to you. Dear children, I want each one of you to open your heart to Jesus and I will give Him to you with love. Dear children, I want Him to change you, to teach you and to protect you. Today I am praying in a special way for each one of you and I am presenting you to God so He will manifest Himself in you. I am calling you to sincere prayer with the heart so that every prayer of yours may be an encounter with God. In your work and in your everyday life, put God in the first place. I call you today with great seriousness to obey me and to do as I am calling you. Thank you for having responded to my call.

***May the eyes of your hearts be enlightened, that you may know what is the hope that belongs to His call, what are the riches of glory in His inheritance among the holy ones, and what is the surpassing greatness of His power for us who believe, in accord with the exercise of His great might.*(Ephesians 1: 18-19)**

Reflection: Mary, I experience your influence daily as a result of my surrender to your call. I see and understand your influence more clearly in my life. You truly are an extension of God's grace and a very real presence in the lives of those who accept you in their hearts. I believe Jesus is very pleased by those who honor and love His Mother.

January 25, 1988

Dear children! Today again I am calling you to complete conversion, which is difficult for those who have not chosen God. God can give you everything that you seek from Him. But you seek God only when sicknesses, problems and difficulties come to you and you think that God is far from you and is not listening and does not hear your prayers. No, dear children, that is not the truth. When you are far from God, you cannot receive graces because you do not seek them with a firm faith. Day by day, I am praying for you, and I want to draw you ever more near to God, but I cannot if you don't want it. Therefore, dear children put your life in God's hands. I bless you all. Thank you for having responded to my call.

I tell you the truth, unless you change and become like little children, you will never enter the kingdom of heaven. Therefore, whoever humbles himself like this child is the greatest in the kingdom of heaven. And whoever welcomes a little child like this in My name welcomes Me. (Matthew 17:20-21)

Reflection: When I see small children it reminds me that I must be like a child within my heart. Help me O God to always be conscious of the importance of childlike faith, with innocent trust and faith in You.

February 25, 1988

Dear children, Today again I am calling you to prayer to complete surrender to God. You know that I love you and am coming here out of love so I could show you the path to peace and salvation for your souls. I want you to obey me and not permit Satan to seduce you. Dear children, Satan is very strong and, therefore, I ask you to dedicate your prayers to me so that those who are under his influence can be saved. Give witness by your life. Sacrifice your lives for the salvation of the world. I am with you, and I am grateful to you, but in heaven you shall receive the Father's reward which He has promised to you. Therefore, dear children, do not be afraid. If you pray, Satan cannot injure you even a little bit because you are God's children and He is watching over you. Pray and let the rosary always be in your hand as a sign to Satan that you belong to me. Thank you for having responded to my call.

Though you have not seen Him, you love Him; and even though you do not see Him now, you believe in Him and are filled with an inexpressible and glorious joy, for you are receiving the goal of your faith, the salvation of your souls. (1 Peter 1: 8-9)

Reflection: God, it gives me great joy and comfort that You would care enough about us to send Your Mother to remind us of the importance of salvation. I thank You for sending Your Son to give us the path of salvation. O God, it is obvious that You had a mysterious plan from the beginning with the use of Your Mother for this world. Thank You for sending her now.

March 25, 1988

Dear children! Today also I am inviting you to a complete surrender to God. Dear children, you are not conscious of how God loves you with such a great love because He permits me to be with you so I can instruct you and help you to find the way of peace. This way, however, you cannot discover if you do not pray. Therefore, dear children, forsake everything and consecrate your time to God and God will bestow gifts upon you and bless you. Little children, don't forget that your life is fleeting like a spring flower which today is wondrously beautiful but tomorrow has vanished. Therefore, pray in such a way that your prayer, your surrender to God, may become like a road sign. That way, your witness will not only have value for yourselves but for all eternity. Thank you for having responded to my call.

This is how God showed His love among us: He sent His one and only Son into the world that we might live through Him. This is love: not that we loved God, but that he loved us and sent His Son as an atoning sacrifice for our sins. Dear friends, since God so loved us, we also ought to love one another. No one has ever seen God; but if we love each other, God lives in us and His love is made complete in us.(1 John 4: 9-12)

Reflection: The voice of wisdom and instruction is coming through the Blessed Lady to the world. It is no wonder that her presence is being felt throughout the world, especially when she had as her Spouse the Holy Spirit! Help me to listen carefully.

April 25, 1988

Dear children! God wants to make you holy. Therefore, through me He is inviting you to complete surrender. Let holy mass be your life. Understand that the church is God's palace, the place in which I gather you and want to show you the way to God. Come and pray. Neither look at others nor slander them, but rather, let your life be a testimony on the way of holiness. Churches deserve respect and are set apart as holy because God, who became man, dwells in them day and night. Therefore, little children, believe and pray that the Father increase your faith, and then ask for whatever you need. I am with you and I am rejoicing because of your conversion and I am protecting you with my motherly mantle. Thank you for having responded to my call

This is the assurance in approaching God: that if we ask anything according to His Will, He hears us. And if we know that he hears us – whatever we ask – we know that we have what we asked of Him. (1 John 5: 14-15)

Reflection: Blessed Lady, you remind us that Mass is a holy event. You are waking many to the holiness of the Mass. I pray that those who do not worship God in Holy Mass will still see you, Blessed Lady, as the heavenly Mother of us all. You are a Heavenly Mother to help and guide, teach and nourish us. You as a Heavenly Mother care for us as your children this way.

May 25, 1988

Dear children! I am inviting you to a complete surrender to God. Pray, little children, that Satan may not carry you about like the branches in the wind. Be strong in God. I desire that through you the whole world may get to know the God of joy. By your life bear witness for God's joy. Do not be anxious nor worried. God himself will help you and show you the way. I desire that you love all men with my love. Only in that way can love reign over the world. Little children, you are mine. I love you and want you to surrender to me so that I can lead you to God. Never cease praying so that Satan cannot take advantage of you. Pray for the knowledge that you are mine. I bless you with blessings of joy. Thank you for having responded to my call.

Now the parable is this: The seed is the Word of God. Those by the wayside are they that hear; then cometh the devil, and taketh away the word out of their hearts, lest they should believe and be saved. (Luke 8:11-12)

Reflection: Blessed Lady, You make clear that Satan is a real force in this world today. With Your grace O God I will prepare my heart like a farmer would prepare the soil then, when I hear Your words, they will take root in my heart. In this way the ways of Satan and the world will not steal that which has been planted deep within me. Help me to plant Your words of Scripture and Your Mother's messages deeply.

June 25, 1988

Dear children! I am calling you to that love which is loyal and pleasing to God. Little children, love bears everything bitter and difficult for the sake of Jesus who is love. Therefore, dear children, pray that God come to your aid, not however according to your desire, but according to His love. Surrender yourself to God so that He may hear you, console you and forgive everything inside you which is a hindrance on the way of love. In this way God can move your life, and you will grow in love. Dear children, glorify God with a hymn of love so that God's love may be able to grow in you day by day to its fullness. Thank you for having responded to my call.

This is how we know what love is: Jesus Christ laid down his life for us. And we ought to lay down our lives for our brothers. If anyone has material possessions and sees his brother in need but has no pity on him, how can the love of God be in him? Dear children, let us not love with words or tongue but with action and in truth. This then is how we know we belong to the truth, and how we set our hearts at rest in His presence whenever our hearts condemn us. For God is greater than our hearts, and He knows everything. (1 John 3:16-20)

Reflection: Lord, I now surrender time, talent and treasure to Your glory. Let my actions serve as a witness of my love for You. Today I will make a conscious decision again for You. Fill me with psalms of praise to glorify Your Name. Use me!

July 25, 1988

Dear children! Today I am calling you to a complete surrender to God. Everything you do and everything you possess give over to God so that He can take control in your life as the King of all that you possess. That way, through me, God can lead you into the depths of the spiritual life. Little children, do not be afraid, because I am with you even if you think there is no way out and that Satan is in control. I am bringing peace to you I am your mother, the Queen of Peace. I am blessing you with the blessings of joy so that for you God may be everything in your life. Thank you for having responded to my call.

Commit your way to the Lord; trust in Him and He will do this: he will make your righteousness shine like the dawn, the justice of your cause like the noonday sun.
(Psalm. 37: 5-6)

Reflection: Lord, there is nothing in this world that compares to the joy and privilege of serving You. Whatever part I play in this marvelous Salvation plan, may I be given the grace, courage and love to follow. I am joyful in understanding the important role Your Mother is playing. Time unfolds many mysteries.

August 25, 1988

Dear children! Today I invite you all to rejoice in the life which God gives you. Little children, rejoice in God, the Creator, because He has created you so wonderfully. Pray that your life be joyful thanksgiving which flows out of your heart like a river of joy. Little children, give thanks unceasingly for all that you possess, for each little gift which God has given you, so that a joyful blessing always comes down from God upon your life. Thank you for having responded to my call.

Be joyful always, pray continually; give thanks in all circumstances, for this is God's Will for you in Christ Jesus.(1 Thessalonians. 5:16-18)

Reflection: The greatest joy I receive is that of giving to others the gifts You give to me. Use me, Lord, to heighten the awareness in others that You are joy. My happiness is deepened with the knowledge that Mary, Your Mother, is near.

September 25, 1988

Dear children! Today I am inviting all of you, without exception, to the way of holiness in your life. God gave you the grace, the gift of holiness. Pray that you may, more and more, comprehend it, and in that way, you will be able, by your life, to bear witness for God. Dear children, I am blessing you and I intercede to God for you so that your way and your witness may be a complete one and a joy for God. Thank you for having responded to my call.

He commissioned us to preach to the people and testify that he is the One appointed by God as judge of the living and the dead. To Him all the prophets bear witness, that everyone who believes in Him will receive forgiveness of sins through His name. (Acts 10:42-43)

Reflection: I fully believe and understand the words that Jesus Christ tells me. He truly is the Way, the Truth, and the Life. Blessed Lady, I realize, also, that your entire mission throughout time has been to make the world aware of this important fact. Thank you for reminding us of this fact and caring for our salvation. Your role as prophet bears witness to your Son, the Father and the Holy Spirit in a special way.

October 25, 1988

Dear children! My invitation that you live the messages which I am giving you is a daily one, specially, little children, because I want to draw you closer to the Heart of Jesus. Therefore, little children, I am inviting you today to the prayer of consecration to Jesus, my dear Son, so that each of you may be His. And then I am inviting you to the consecration of my Immaculate Heart. I want you to consecrate yourselves as parents, as families and as parishioners so that all belong to God through my heart. Therefore, little children, pray that you comprehend the greatness of this message which I am giving you. I do not want anything for myself, rather all for the salvation of your soul. Satan is strong and therefore, you, little children, by constant prayer, press tightly against my motherly heart. Thank you for having responded to my call.

The Lord is my strength and my shield. My heart trusts in Him and I am helped. My heart leaps for joy and I will give thanks to Him in song. The Lord is the strength of his people, a fortress of salvation for His anointed one. (Psalm 28:7-8)

Reflection: Today, I consecrate my family, myself, all those who are close to me and all of my works to the Immaculate Heart of Mary and the Sacred Heart of Jesus. I realize and trust the importance of performing this Act of Consecration even though I cannot directly see its full meaning. In faith, I follow Your Two Hearts.

November 25, 1988

Dear children! I call you to prayer, to have an encounter with God in prayer. God gives Himself to you, but He wants you to answer in your own freedom to his invitation. That is why little children during the day, find yourself a special time when you could pray in peace and humility, and have this meeting with God the creator. I am with you and I intercede for you in front of God, so watch in vigil, so that every encounter in prayer be the joy of your contact with God. Thank you for having responded to my call.

But I call to God, and the Lord saves me. Evening, morning and noon I cry out in distress, and he hears my voice. He ransoms me unharmed from the battle waged against me, even though many oppose me.
(Psalm 55: 16-18)

Reflection: Each day I get renewed in grace when I take the time to pray. Even if it is just a short prayer, God knows I'm thinking of Him. Thank you, God, for this increased joy in discovering the power of prayer. I pray constantly for your intercession, Lady of Medjugorje, in the lives of my family members and those you have me pray for.

December 25, 1988

Dear children! I call you to peace. Live it in your heart and all around you, so that all will know peace, peace that does not come from you but from God. Little children, today is a great day. Rejoice with me. Glorify the Nativity of Jesus through the peace that I give you. It is for this peace that I have come as your Mother, Queen of Peace. Today I give you my special blessing. Bring it to all creation, so that all creation will know peace. Thank you for having responded to my call.

***Therefore, since we have been justified through faith, we have peace with God through Our Lord Jesus Christ, through Whom we have gained access by faith into this grace in which we now stand.* (Romans 5:1-2)**

Reflection: Today I will do what I can to play a part in spreading the peace which God brings to me. I will use my gifts and talents for peace. Today, again, I am Your servant. For the sake of peace I meditate upon the Immaculate Heart of Mary. I especially pray for the conversion of Russia as she requested at Fatima, Portugal in 1917. Fatima is not completed yet!

January 25, 1989

Dear children! Today I am calling you to the way of holiness. Pray that you may comprehend the beauty and the greatness of this way where God reveals himself to you in a special way. Pray that you may be open to everything that God does through you that in your life you may be enabled to give thanks to God and to rejoice over everything that He does through each individual. I give you my blessing. Thank you for having responded to my call.

Each one should use whatever gift he has received to serve others, faithfully administering God's graces in its various forms. If anyone speaks, he should do it as one speaking the very words of God. If anyone serves, he should do it with the strength God provides, so that in all things God may be praised through Jesus Christ. To Him be the glory and the power forever and ever. Amen.
(1 Peter 4: 4-11)

Reflection: I want to thank You, Lord, for the many gifts which You have bestowed on us. Create in us a desire to use them for You. Help us to understand that true joy is experienced when these gifts are returned to You. Strengthen and protect us in the battle that rages on against Your Kingdom.

February 25, 1989

Dear children! Today I invite you to prayer of the heart. Throughout this season of grace I wish each of you to be united with Jesus, but without unceasing prayer you cannot experience the beauty and greatness of the grace which God is offering you. Therefore, little children, at all times fill your heart with even the smallest prayers. I am with you and unceasingly keep watch over every heart which is given to me. Thank you for having responded to my call.

And pray in the Spirit on all occasions with all kinds of prayers and requests. With this in mind, be alert and always keep on praying for all the saints.
(Ephesians 6:18)

Reflection: Let all that I do be a form of prayer offered to You. Blessed Lady, you are with me, praying with me as I raise my form of prayer to God. May all I do today be pleasing to the Father.

March 25, 1989

Dear children! I am calling you to a complete surrender to God. I am calling you to great joy and peace which only God can give. I am with you and I intercede for you every day before God. I call you, little children, to listen to me and to live the messages that I am giving you. Already for years you are invited to holiness but you are still far away. I am blessing you. Thank you for having responded to my call.

As obedient children, do not conform to the evil desires you had when you lived in ignorance. But just as He who called you is Holy, so be holy in all you do; for it is written: Be holy, because I am Holy. (1 Peter 1:14-16)

Reflection: Blessed Lady, you make it clear that you intercede to the Lord on my behalf. Although my human nature is as a sinner, your influence brings me to the cross of your Son, where reconciliation and purification precedes holiness. Keep me always centered on your Son and His Words.

April 25, 1989

Dear children! I am calling you to a complete surrender to God. Let everything that you possess be in the hands of God. Only in that way shall you have joy in your heart. Little children, rejoice in everything that you have. Give thanks to God because everything is God's gift to you. That way in your life you shall be able to give thanks for everything and discover God in everything even in the smallest flower. Thank you for having responded to my call

Speak to one another with psalms, hymns and spiritual songs. Sing and make music in your heart to the Lord, always giving thanks to God, the Father, for everything, in the name of Our Lord Jesus Christ.(Ephesians 5:19-20)

Reflection: I thank you, God, for the great gift of music. I share it with others so that Your love can penetrate more deeply into their hearts and cause their faith to rise. Fill me, O God, with Your music and I shall pass it on with great joy.

May 25, 1989

Dear children! I invite you now to be open to God. See, children, how nature is opening herself and is giving life and fruits. In the same way I invite you to live with God and to surrender completely to him. Children, I am with you and I want to introduce you continuously to the joy of life. I desire that everyone may discover the joy and love which can be found only in God and which only God can give. God doesn't want anything from you only your surrender. Therefore, children, decide seriously for God because everything else passes away. Only God doesn't pass away. Pray to be able to discover the greatness and joy of life which God gives you. Thank you for having responded to my call.

Then Jesus said to His disciples, "If anyone would come after me, he must deny himself and take up his cross and follow Me. For whoever wants to save his life will lose it, but whoever loses his life for me will find it. What good will it be for a man if he gains the whole world, yet forfeits his soul? Or what can a man give in exchange for his soul? (Matthew 16:24-26)

Reflection: Time is quickly passing. Mary, by echoing your Son's words, you make it clear that time is fleeting. You urge us to be aware that what we do here on earth for God can affect our eternal existence. My surrender is what God desires. It is through this surrender the joy of life can be seen. Thank you for allowing me to experience this mystery.

June 25, 1989

Dear children! Today I am calling you to live the messages I have been giving you during the past eight years. This is the time of grace and I desire the grace of God be great for every single one of you. I am blessing you and I love you with a special love. Thank you for having responded to call.

For we do not have a high priest who is unable to sympathize our weaknesses, but we have one who has been tempted in every way, just as we are – yet was without sin. Let us then approach the throne of grace with confidence, so that we may receive mercy and find grace to help us in our time of need. (Hebrews 4:15-16)

Reflection: You have been sent by God, Blessed Lady, as His instrument guiding and instructing us in His light. You have told us that everything you do in the Spirit is God's Will. I believe that soon all will know the power invested in you from God. You were His special vessel over 2,000 years ago, and you bring us His Good News again today. You have been presenting your Son over and over throughout the centuries. It would make perfect sense that you who brought the Christ into this world would be the same instrument to prepare His return.

July 25, 1989

Dear children! Today I am calling you to renew your hearts. Open yourselves to God and surrender to him all your difficulties and crosses so, God may turn everything into joy. Little children, you cannot open yourselves to God if you do not pray. Therefore, from today, decide to consecrate a time in the day only for an encounter with God in silence. In that way you will be able, with God, to witness my presence here. Little children, I do not wish to force you. Rather freely give God your time, like children of God. Thank you for having responded to my call.

You were taught, with regard to your former way of life, to put your old self, which is being corrupted by its deceitful desires; to be made new in the attitude of your minds; and to put on the new self, created to be like God in true righteousness and holiness. (Ephesians 4:22-24)

Reflection: This world will always have trials and tribulations. The more I recognize and accept this fact the more I submit all of my cares into Your hands. I commit my ways unto You. You know far greater than I what is best for my life. So I trust You, God, to lead me to glory.

August 25, 1989

Dear children! I call you to prayer. By means of prayer, little children, you obtain joy and peace. Through prayer you are richer in the mercy of God. Therefore, little children, let prayer be the life of each one of you. Especially I call you to pray so that all those who are far away from God may be converted. Then our hearts shall be richer because God will rule in the hearts of all men. Therefore, little children, pray, pray, pray! Let prayers begin to rule in the whole world. Thank you for having responded to my call.

Give ear to my words, O Lord, consider my meditation. Hearken unto the voice of my cry, my King and my God. For unto Thee I will pray. My voice shalt thou hear in the morning, O Lord; in the morning will I direct my prayer unto thee, and will look up. (Psalm 5:1-3)

Reflection: By prayer I will receive joy and peace. Your light is getting brighter, ever growing, getting stronger. I accept in faith this mystery of finding joy and peace in prayer. I offer You my prayer today for peace in the world and for the conversion of sinners.

September 25, 1989

Dear children! Today I invite you to give thanks to God for all the gifts you have discovered in the course of your life and even for the least gift that you have perceived. I give thanks with you and want all of you to experience the joy of these gifts. And I want God to be everything for each one of you. And then, little children, you can grow continuously on the way of holiness. Thank you for responding to my call.

There are different kinds of gifts, but the same Spirit. There are different kinds of service, but the same Lord. There are different kinds of workings, but the same God works all of them in all men. **(1 Corinthians 12: 4-5)**

Reflection: Lord God, You are the great giver of all good gifts. Help us to be mindful that these gifts are to be used to build up the Body of Christ. I praise You for even the smallest of gifts and even that smallest of gift can be of great use when used for You. No gift is too small when used in Your name and for the edification of Your Church.

October 25, 1989

Dear children! Today also I am inviting you to prayer. I am always inviting you, but you are still far away. Therefore, from today, decide seriously to dedicate time to God. I am with you and I wish to teach you to pray with the heart. In prayer with the heart you shall encounter God. Therefore, little children, pray, pray, pray! Thank you for having responded to my call.

But the Lord said to Samuel, "Do not consider his appearance or his height, for I have rejected him. The Lord does not look at the things man looks at. Man looks at the outward appearances, but the Lord looks at the heart." (1 Samuel 16:7)

Reflection: It's amazing to me that the Blessed Lady often speaks of the heart in her messages. I see the words to Samuel. It is evident that what is in the heart is important to God.

Create a clean heart, O Lord, in me!

November 25, 1989

Dear children! I am inviting you for years by these messages which I am giving you. Little children, by means of the messages I wish to make a very beautiful mosaic in your hearts, so I may be able to present each one of you to God like the original image. Therefore, little children, I desire that your decisions be free before God, because He has given you freedom. Therefore pray, so that, free from any influence of Satan, we may decide only for God. I am praying for you before God and I am seeking your surrender to God. Thank you for responding to my call.

Delight yourself in the Lord and He will give you the desires of your heart. Commit your way to the Lord. Trust in Him and He will do this: He will make your righteousness shine like the dawn, the justice of your cause like the noonday sun.(Psalm 37:4-6)

Reflection: As I learn the meaning of surrender, I begin to comprehend that the ways of God are not like the ways of man. In order to conform to His ways a willful act of surrender to His Will is needed. Then I begin to see my decisions more clearly and truth more clearly.

December 25, 1989

*Dear children! Today I bless you in a special way with my motherly blessing and I am interceding for you before God that He gives you the gift of conversion of the heart. For years I am calling you and exhorting you to a deep spiritual life in simplicity, but you are so cold. Therefore, little children, I ask you to accept and **<u>live the messages</u>** with seriousness, so that your soul will not be sad when I will no longer be with you, and when I will no longer lead you like insecure children in their first steps. Therefore, little children, every day read the messages that I have given you and transform them into life. I love you and therefore I am calling you all to the way of salvation with God. Thank you for having responded to my call.*

It is by the name of Jesus Christ of Nazareth, whom you crucified, but whom God raised from the dead, that this man stands before you healed. He is "the stone you builders rejected, which has become the cornerstone." Salvation is found in no one else, for there is no other name under heaven given to men by which we must be saved. (Acts 4:10-12)

<u>Reflection:</u> The Blessed Lady knows that the way of salvation is through no other than her Son, Jesus Christ. She is always calling and praying all will respond.

January 25, 1990

Dear children!, Today I invite you to decide for God once again and to choose Him before everything and above everything, so that He may work miracles in your life and that day by day your life may become joy with Him. Therefore, little children, pray and do not permit Satan to work in your life through misunderstandings, the non-understanding and non-acceptance of one another. Pray that you may be able to comprehend the greatness and the beauty of the gift of life. Thank you for having responded to my call.

Then Jesus said to them, "Don't you understand this parable? How then will you understand any parable? The farmer sows the word. Some people are like seed on the path, where the word is sown. As soon as they hear it, Satan comes and takes away the word that was sown in them." (Mark 4:13-15)

Reflection: I am beginning to see how you influence the faith in every age. Why every age shall call you Blessed, because you are always illuminating the world to the very real powers of Satan and evil. From the very Scripture of Genesis 3:15 you have been in battle with your adversary Satan. Help me to be good seed that falls on fertile soil and produces abundantly.

February 25, 1990

Dear children! I invite you to surrender to God. In this season I specially want you to renounce all the things to which you are attached but which are hurting your spiritual life. Therefore, little children, decide completely for God, and do not allow Satan to come into your life through those things that hurt both you and your spiritual life. Little children, God is offering Himself to you in His fullness, and you can discover and recognize Him only in prayer. Therefore make a decision for prayer. Thank you for having responded to my call.

Let your gentleness be evident to all. The Lord is near. Do not be anxious about anything, but in everything, by prayer and petition, with thanksgiving, present your requests to God. And the peace of God, which transcends all understanding, will guard your hearts and your minds in Jesus Christ. (Philippians 4: 5-7)

Reflection: Mary, you continue to remind us so often of the importance of prayer, and here we see it in Scripture clearly. Everything moves so fast in this world and we tire in trying to keep up with it. It is through prayer we are refreshed. Our anxieties are not as great when we place them in God's hands.

March 25, 1990

Dear children, I am with you even if you are not conscious of it. I want to protect you from everything that Satan offers you and through which he wants to destroy you. As I bore Jesus in my womb, so also, dear children, do I wish to bear you into holiness. God wants to save you and sends you messages through men, nature, and so many things which can only help you to understand that you must change the direction of your life. Therefore, little children, understand also the greatness of the gift which God is giving you through me, so that I may protect you with my mantle and lead you to the joy of life. Thank you for having responded to my call.

My soul glorifies the Lord and my spirit rejoices in God my Savior, for He has been mindful of the humble state of His servant. From now on all generations shall call me blessed, for the Mighty One has done great things for me-holy is His name. (Luke 1:46-49)

Reflection: Wherever you appear you are always birthing Jesus into the hearts of many. Wherever you appear many are presented with the grace of conversion. I desire you as my heavenly Mother and I ask you for your protection as your child.

April 25, 1990

*Dear children! Today I invite you to accept with seriousness and to **live the messages** which I am giving you. I am with you and I desire, dear children, that each one of you be ever closer to my heart. Therefore, little children, pray and seek the will of God in your everyday life. I desire that each one of you discover the way of holiness and grow in it until eternity. I will pray for you and intercede for you before God that you understand the greatness of this gift which God is giving me that I can be with you. Thank you for having responded to my call.*

Peter replied, "Repent and be baptized, every one of you, in the name of Jesus Christ for the forgiveness of your sins. And you will receive the gift of the Holy Spirit. The promise is for you and your children and for all who are far off-for all whom the Lord our God will call."
(Acts 2:38-39)

Reflection: Blessed Lady, you ask that we seek the Will of God in everyday life. The Holy Spirit is the great assistance we have to help us through this life. You have said that with the Holy Spirit we have everything.

May 25, 1990

Dear children! I invite you to decide with seriousness to live this novena. Consecrate the time to prayer and to sacrifice. I am with you and I desire to help you to grow in renunciation and mortification that you may be able to understand the beauty of the life of people who go on giving themselves to me in special ways. Dear children, God blesses you day after day and desires a change of your life. Therefore, pray that you may have the strength to change your life. Thank you for having responded to my call.

I urge you therefore, brothers, by the mercies of God, to offer your bodies as a living sacrifice, holy and pleasing to God, your spiritual worship. Do not conform yourself to this age, but be transformed by the renewal of your mind, that you may discern what is the will of God, what is good and pleasing and perfect. (Romans 12:1-2)

Reflection: It's a mystery how the Blessed Virgin Mary is always asking for prayers and sacrifices. She has stated that the graces she receives from God, she receives through prayer. As children of Mary, it appears she is increasingly empowered by our prayers and sacrifices. She also stated that if we knew the results of our prayers we would want to pray all the time. Let us believe that our prayers produce results.

June 25, 1990

Dear children! Today I desire to thank you for all your sacrifices and for all your prayers. I am blessing you with my special motherly blessing. I invite you all to decide for God, so that from day to day you will discover His will in prayer. I desire, dear children, to call all of you to a full conversion so that joy will be in your hearts. I am happy that you are here today in such great numbers. Thank you for having responded to my call

**We have not received the spirit of the world, but the Spirit of God, so that we may understand the things freely given us by God. And we speak about them not with words taught with human wisdom, but with words taught by the Spirit, describing spiritual realities in spiritual terms.
(1 Corinthians 3:12-13)**

Reflection: With her words we are listening to words from heaven. Mary, now a supernatural being **speaks to us** through the Holy Spirit. To have been one of the 250,000 people seeing her at one time in Zeitun, Egypt, with nearly all nationalities and religions must be unforgettable. Let us have the faith to believe God sends His Mother now and let us discover for ourselves, what that means for each and every one of us in prayer.

July 25, 1990

Dear children! Today I invite you to peace. I have come here as the Queen of Peace and I desire to enrich you with my motherly peace. Dear children, I love you and I desire to bring all of you to the peace which only God gives and which enriches every heart. I invite you to become carriers and witnesses of my peace to this unpeaceful world. Let peace reign in the whole world which is without peace and longs for peace. I bless you with my motherly blessing. Thank you for having responded to my call.

Have no anxiety at all, but in everything, by prayer and petition, with thanksgiving, make your requests known to God. And the peace of God, that surpasses all understanding, will guard your hearts and minds in Christ Jesus. (Philippians 4:7)

Reflection: This mystery of Mary's appearances around the world is playing itself out. Peace is being disrupted in nearly every segment of society. Let us believe that our prayers will lead to peace in our own hearts and then lead to peace in our families and the world.

August 25, 1990

*Dear children, I desire to invite you to take with seriousness and put into practice the messages which I am giving you. You know, little children, that I am with you and I desire to lead you along the same path to heaven, which is beautiful for those who discover it in prayer. Therefore, little children, do not forget that those messages which I am giving you have to be put into your everyday life in order that you might be able to say: "There, I have taken the messages and **tried to live them**." Dear children, I am protecting you before the heavenly Father by my own prayers. Thank you for having responded to my call.*

Every athlete exercises discipline in every way. They do it to win a perishable crown, but we an imperishable one. (1 Corinthians 9:25)

Reflection: It takes discipline, like a training athlete to take time to pray and to live these messages. When I carry my Rosary on me I am reminded to take some time and pray. When I pray the Rosary I recall many of your messages. Then I am in tune to setting myself to living them. It is a daily decision, but I know it is important to try my best.

September 1990

Dear children, I invite you to pray with the heart in order that your prayer may be a conversation with God. I desire each one of you to dedicate more time to God. Satan is strong and wants to destroy and deceive you in many ways. Therefore, dear children, pray every day that your life will be good for yourselves and for all those you meet. I am with you and I am protecting you even though Satan wishes to destroy my plans and to hinder the desires which the Heavenly Father wants to realize here. Thank you for having responded to my call.

No trial has come to you but what is human. God is faithful and will not let you be tried beyond your strength; but with the trial He will also provide a way out so that you may be able to bear it. (1 Corinthians 10:13)

Reflection: I became acquainted with this passage of Scripture early in my life. We must have faith to believe that God is always there to help us make the right decisions. When confronted with evil or sin this passage has come to mind. It is a recommended passage to put to memory. This is how the Holy Spirit uses Holy Scripture. He will bring it back to our memory when most needed.

October 25, 1990

Dear children! Today I call you to pray in a special way that you offer up sacrifices and good deeds for peace in the world. Satan is strong and with all his strength, desires to destroy the peace which comes from God. Therefore, dear children, pray in a special way with me for peace. I am with you and I desire to help you with my prayers and I desire to guide you on the path of peace. I bless you with my motherly blessing. Do not forget to live the messages of peace. Thank you for having responded to my call.

Keep your tongue from evil and your lips from speaking guile. Turn from evil and do good; seek peace and follow after it. The Lord has eyes for the just and ears for their cry. The Lord confronts the evil doers, to destroy remembrance of them from the earth.
(Psalm 34:14-17)

Reflection: One thing for sure is that this Blessed Lady is impressing on our minds that the battle between Satan and God is real. This is the ultimate spiritual reality in the world. This evil manifests itself in many ways in our world. Let us become consciously aware and then allow God to engage us with prayer. Remember she said at Fatima "In the end My Immaculate Heart shall triumph!"

November 25, 1990

Dear children! Today I invite you to do works of mercy with love and out of love for me and for your and my brothers and sisters. Dear children, all that you do for others, do it with great joy and humility towards God. I am with you and day after day I offer your sacrifices and prayers to God for the salvation of the world. Thank you for having responded to my call.

Be doers of the word and not hearers only, deluding yourselves. For if anyone is a hearer of the word and not a doer, he is like a man who looks at his own face in a mirror. He sees himself then goes off and forgets what he looked like. But the one who peers into the perfect law of freedom and perseveres, and is not a hearer who forgets but a doer who acts, such a one shall be blessed in what he does.(James 2:22-25)

Reflection: James, in Scripture, exhorts us to good works. It is not enough to become aware of what is happening in Medjugorje. If we have faith to believe Mary is here for our good, then we must try to follow her advice. Scripture supports her words. Let us be guided by the same Holy Spirit that brings these words from heaven, and follow with action.

December 25, 1990

Dear children! Today I invite you in a special way to pray for peace. Dear children, without peace you cannot experience the birth of the little Jesus neither today nor in your daily lives. Therefore, pray the Lord of Peace that He may protect you with His mantle and that He may help you to comprehend the greatness and the importance of peace in your heart. In this way you shall be able to spread peace from your heart throughout the whole world. I am with you and I intercede for you before God. Pray, because Satan wants to destroy my plans of peace. Be reconciled with one another and by means of your lives help peace reign in the whole earth. Thank you for having responded to my call.

For the kingdom of God is not a matter of food and drink, but of righteousness, peace, and joy in the Holy spirit; whoever serves Christ in this way is pleasing to God and approved by others. Let us then pursue what leads to peace and to building up one another.
(Romans 14:17-19)

Reflection: The kind of peace that passes all understanding is a divine peace and does not come from this world. In Fatima, the Angel of Peace preceded Our Lady, and he taught the three children this prayer. He prayed this three times: **"O my God, I believe, I adore, I hope and I love You. I beg pardon of You for those who do not believe, do not adore, do not hope and do not love You."** Thank You, God, for showing me this prayer. I will pray it often.

January 25, 1991

Dear children! Today, like never before, I invite you to prayer. Let your prayer be a prayer for peace. Satan is strong and desires to destroy not only human life, but also nature and the planet on which you live. Therefore, dear children, pray that through prayer you can protect yourselves with God's blessing of peace. God has sent me among you so that I may help you. If you so wish, grasp for the rosary. Even the rosary alone can work miracles in the world and in your lives. I bless you and I remain with you for as long as it is God's will. Thank you for not betraying my presence here and I thank you because your response is serving the good and the peace. Thank you for having responded to my call.

Put on the armor of God so that you may be able to stand firm against the tactics of the devil. For our struggle is not with flesh and blood but with the principalities, with the powers, with the world rulers of this present darkness, with the evil spirits in the heavens.
(Ephesians 6:11-12)

Reflection: The power of the Rosary is illuminated in Mary's words. The Rosary is becoming more and more prayed. The Rosary is a scriptural prayer made up of the Lord's own prayer, The Our Father, while the "Hail Mary's" are from the accounts of the angel's visit to Mary (the Annunciation) in Luke's Gospel. Let us believe in her words that the Rosary is for our own good and protection. She said it is the prayer that Satan runs from.

February 25, 1991

Dear children! Today, I invite you to decide for God, because distance from God is the fruit of the lack of peace in your hearts. God is only peace. Therefore, approach Him through your personal prayer and then live peace in your hearts and in this way peace will flow from your hearts like a river into the whole world. Do not talk about peace, but make peace. I am blessing each of you and each good decision of yours. Thank you for having responded to my call.

May the God of peace, who brought up from the dead the great shepherd of the sheep by the blood of the eternal covenant, Jesus our Lord, furnish you with all that is good, that you may do His Will. (Hebrews 13:20-21)

Reflection: It is like discovering the "great pearl" to discover God's Holy Will for our lives. To those who earnestly seek, knock and ask, with all sincerity to discover it, God will reveal it. To discover it leads to lasting peace in the heart. Help me, O God, to be steadfast in my commitment to Your Holy Will in my life.

March 25, 1991

Dear children! Again today I invite you to live the passion of Jesus in prayer and in union with Him. Decide to give more time to God who gave you these days of grace. Therefore, dear children, pray and in a special way renew the love for Jesus for in your hearts. I am with you and I accompany you with my blessing any my prayers. Thank you for having responded to my call.

...and that Christ may dwell in your hearts through faith; that you, rooted and grounded in love, may have the strength to comprehend with all the holy ones what is the breadth and length and height and depth, and to know the love of Christ that surpasses knowledge, so that you may be filled with all the fullness of God.
(Ephesians 3:17-19)

Reflection: The everyday pressures and responsibilities of life are difficult for many today. We must discipline ourselves to take time and pray. God will surely help us in our daily struggles. They will become more manageable, because the light of Christ will begin to guide us and protect us. God will also begin to show us the things that are meaningless. We will begin to see the things that really matter….. Communion with Him

April 25, 1991

Dear children! Today I invite you all so that your prayer be prayer with the heart. Let each of you find time for prayer so that in prayer you discover God. I do not desire you to talk about prayer, but to pray. Let your every day be filled with prayer of gratitude to God for life and for all that you have. I do not desire your life to pass by in words but that you glorify God with deeds. I am with you and I am grateful to God for every moment spent with you. Thank you for having responded to my call.

For just as a body without a spirit is dead, so also faith without works is dead. (James 2:26)

Reflection: Isn't it amazing that Our Lady expresses how thankful she is to God that she has time to spend with us. It is clear in those words that it is God who controls her time here on earth. One day she will be gone. Remember she says this is her last time here on earth. Let us listen to what she speaks and take it to heart. Let the Spirit of God reveal to you her tremendous importance while we have her in our midst.

May 25, 1991

Dear Children, Today I invite all of you who have heard my message of peace to realize it with seriousness and with love in your life. There are many who think that they are doing a lot by talking about the messages, but do not live them. Dear children, I invite you to life and to change all the negative in you, so that it all turns into the positive and life. Dear children, I am with you and I desire to help each of you to live and by living, to witness the good news. I am here, dear children, to help you and to lead you to heaven, and in heaven is the joy through which you can already live heaven now. Thank you for having responded to my call.

For you were once darkness, but now you are light in the Lord. Live as children of light, for light produces every kind of goodness and righteousness and truth. Try to learn what is pleasing to the Lord.(Ephesians 5:8-10)

Reflection: Incredible it is that she wants to lead us to heaven. Do you want that? The world and her enemy, Satan, is always wanting to rob us of that goal. We need to make a firm decision to be on the side of God and not Satan. Our Lady promises us that Satan's power is going to be broken soon. Let us believe this and pray for the triumph of her Immaculate Heart.

June 25, 1991

Dear children, Today on this great day which you have given to me, I desire to bless all of you and to say: these days while I am with you are days of grace. I desire to teach you and help you to walk the way of holiness. There are many people who do not desire to understand my messages and to accept with seriousness what I am saying. But you I therefore call and ask that by your lives and by your daily living you witness my presence. If you pray, God will help you to discover the true reason for my coming. Therefore, little children, pray and read the Sacred Scriptures so that through my coming you discover the message in Sacred Scripture for you. Thank you for having responded to my call.

Since you have purified yourselves by obedience to the truth for sincere mutual love, love one another intensely from a pure heart. You have been born anew, not from perishable but imperishable seed, through the living and abiding word of God. (1 Peter 1:22-23)

Reflection: I realize that if I choose holiness, God's Holy Spirit will guide me in that direction and the Blessed Virgin will also be very close to help me on that path. It is the path that leads to lasting peace. How fortunate we are to have this time with the Mother of God: to teach us, guide us, warn us and love us.

(A passage the Virgin Mary urges us to read often)

"No man can serve two masters. He will either hate one and love the other or be attentive to one and despise the other. You cannot give yourself to God and money. I warn you then: do not worry about your livelihood, what you are to eat or drink or use for clothing. Is not life more than food? Is not the body more valuable than clothes? Look at the birds in the sky. They do not sow or reap, they gather nothing into barns; yet your heavenly Father feeds them. Are you not more important than they? Which of you by worrying can add one moment to his life span? As for clothes, why be concerned? Learn a lesson from the way the wild flowers grow. They do not work; they do not spin. Yet, I assure you, not even Solomon in all his splendor was arrayed like one of these. If God can clothe, in such splendor, the grass of the field, which blooms today and is thrown in the fire tomorrow, will He not provide much more for you? O weak in faith! Stop worrying. Then over questions like, 'what are we to eat or what are we to drink, or what are we to wear?' The unbelievers are always running after these things. Your heavenly Father knows all that you need. Seek first His Kingship over you, His way of holiness, and all these things will be given you besides. Enough, then, of worrying about tomorrow. Let tomorrow take care of itself. Today has troubles enough of its own."

(Matthew 6:24-34)

Chapter 4
Medjugorje Our Lady Speaks To The World
Illuminating Messages

Third Day

I am the Blessed Virgin Mary. I have come because there are many true believers. I wish to covert to reconcile people.

Peace, peace, only peace. Reconcile yourselves. Peace must take place between God and man and between men.

Fourth Day

Let those who do not see believe as if they see

Fifth Day

Let these people, who do not see me, believe the same as the six of you who see me.

Sixth Day

There is only one God and one faith. Believe firmly!

Early Days

Pray more and do penance! Wherever God calls you, go!

*I know that many will not believe you and many who are enthusiastic for the faith will grow cold; but you stay steadfast and urge all people to prayer, penance and conversion. **At the end, you will be the happiest.***

Unknown Fire

*This is one of the heralds of the great sign. There will be many more such signs throughout the world, in Medjugorje and other parts of the world, before the **"great sign"**.*

Whenever you have difficulties and need help, come to me.

Many have begun their conversion, but not all.

My beloved Son! Please forgive those numerous serious sins with which humanity offends You.

I cannot heal you. Only God can heal you. But pray to be healed and I will pray with you. Believe firmly, fast, and do penance and I will intercede. God, of course, helps everybody, but I am not God.

About Russia

*It is the people where God will be most glorified. The **West** has made civilization progress, but without God, as if they were their own creators.*

*I have come to call the world to conversion for the **last time**. Later, I will not appear any more on this earth.*

*One must invite people to go to **confession each month**, especially the first Saturday. Here I have not spoken about it yet. I have invited people to frequent confession. I will give you yet some concrete messages for our time. Be patient because the time has not yet come. Do what I have told you. They are numerous who do not observe it. Monthly confession will be a remedy for the Church in the West. One must convey this message to the West.*

August 31, 1982

I do not dispose all graces. I receive them from God what I obtain through prayer. God has placed His complete trust in me. **The great sign has been granted. It will appear independently of the conversion of the people.**

April 25, 1983

Be converted. It will be too late when the sign comes. Beforehand several warnings will be given to the world. Have people hurry to be converted. I need your prayers and your penance. My heart is burning with love for you. It suffices for you to be converted. To ask questions is unimportant. Be converted! Hurry to proclaim it! Tell everyone that it is my wish and that I do not cease repeating it. **Be converted! Be converted!"** *"It is not difficult for me to suffer for you. I beg you be converted. I will pray to my Son to spare you the punishment. Be converted without delay. You do not know the plans of God. You will not be able to know them. You will not know what God will send, nor what He will do. I ask you only to be converted. That is what I wish. Be converted! Be ready for everything, but be converted. That is all I wish to say to you.*

March 25, 1992

Dear children! Today as never before I invite you to **live my messages** *and to put them into practice in your life. I have come to you to help you and, therefore, I invite you to change your life because you have taken a path of misery, a path of ruin. When I told you: convert, pray, fast, be reconciled, you took these messages superficially. You started to live them and then you stopped, because it was difficult for you. No, dear children, when something is good, you have to persevere in the good and not think: 'God does not see* *me, He is not listening, He is not helping'. And so you have gone away from God and from me because of your miserable interest. I wanted to create of you an oasis of peace, love and goodness. God wanted you, with your love and with His help, to do miracles and, thus, give an example. Therefore, here is what I say to you: Satan is playing with you and with your souls and I cannot help you because you are far away from my heart.* **Therefore, pray, live my messages and then you will see the miracles of God's love in your everyday life.** *Thank you for having responded to my call.*

January 25, 1993

Dear children! Today I call you to accept and live my messages with seriousness. These days are the days when you need to decide for God, for peace and for the good. **May every hatred and jealousy disappear from your life and your thoughts, and may there only dwell love for God and for your neighbor.** *Thus, and only thus shall you be able to discern the signs of the time. I am with you and I guide you into a new time, a time which God gives you as grace so that you may get to know him more. Thank you for having responded to my call.*

January 25, 1995

Dear children! I invite you to open the door of your heart to Jesus as the flower opens itself to the sun. Jesus desires to fill your hearts with peace and joy. You cannot, little children, realize peace if you are not at **peace with Jesus**. *Therefore, I invite you to confession so Jesus may be your truth and peace. So, little children, pray to have the strength to realize what I am telling you. I am with you and I love you. Thank you for having responded to my call.*

January 25, 1996

*Dear children! Today I invite you to decide for peace. Pray that God give you the true peace. Live peace in your hearts and you will understand, dear children, that peace is the gift of God. Dear children, without love you cannot live peace. The fruit of peace is love and the fruit of love is **forgiveness**. I am with you and I invite all of you, little children, that before all else forgive in the family and then you will be able to forgive others. Thank you for having responded to my call.*

November 25, 1997

*Dear children! Today I invite you to comprehend your Christian vocation. Little children, I led and am leading you through this time of grace, that you may become conscious of your Christian vocation. Holy martyrs died witnessing: I am a Christian and love God over everything. Little children, today also I invite you to rejoice and be joyful Christians, responsible and conscious that God called you in a special way to be joyfully extended hands toward those who do not believe, and that through the example of your life, they may receive faith and love for God. **Therefore, pray, pray, pray that your heart may open and be sensitive for the Word of God.** Thank you for having responded to my call.*

March 25, 1999

*Dear children! I call you to prayer with the heart. In a special way, little children, I call you to pray for conversion of sinners, for those who pierce my heart and the heart of my Son Jesus with the sword of hatred and daily blasphemies. Let us pray, little children, for all those who do not desire to come to know the love of God, even though they are in the Church. **Let us pray that they convert, so that the Church*** *may resurrect in love. Only with love and prayer, little children, can you live this time which is given to you for conversion. Place God in the first place, then the risen Jesus will become your friend. Thank you for having responded to my call.*

May 25, 2000

Dear children! I rejoice with you and in this time of grace I call you to spiritual renewal. **Pray, little children, that the Holy Spirit may come to dwell in you in fullness, so that you may be able to witness in joy to all those who are far from faith.** *Especially, little children, pray for the gifts of the Holy Spirit so that in the spirit of love, every day and in each situation, you may be closer to your fellow-man; and that in wisdom and love you may overcome every difficulty. I am with you and I intercede for each of you before Jesus. Thank you for having responded to my call.*

January 25, 2001

Dear children! Today I call you to ***renew prayer and fasting*** *with even greater enthusiasm until prayer becomes a joy for you. Little children, the one who prays is not afraid of the future and the one who fasts is not afraid of evil. Once again, I repeat to you: only through prayer and fasting also wars can be stopped - wars of your unbelief and fear for the future. I am with you and am teaching you little children: your peace and hope are in God. That is why draw closer to God and put Him in the first place in your life. Thank you for having responded to my call.*

December 25, 2002

Dear children! This is a time of great graces, but also a time of great trials for all those who desire to follow the way of peace. Because of that, **little children, again I call you to pray, pray, pray, not with words but with the heart. Live my messages and be converted.** *Be conscious of this gift that God has permitted me to be with you, especially today when in my arms I have little Jesus - the King of Peace. I desire to give you peace, and that you carry it in your hearts and give it to others until God's peace begins to rule the world. Thank you for having responded to my call.*

June 25, 2007

Dear children! Also today, with great joy in my heart, I call you to conversion. Little children, do not forget that you are all important in this great plan, which God leads through Medjugorje. **God desires to convert the entire world and to call it to salvation and to the way towards Himself, who is the beginning and the end of every being.** *In a special way, little children, from the depth of my heart, I call you all to open yourselves to this great grace that God gives you through my presence here. I desire to thank each of you for the sacrifices and prayers. I am with you and I bless you all. Thank you for having responded to my call.*

October 25, 2008

Dear children! In a special way I call you all to pray for my intentions so that, through your prayers, you may stop Satan's plan over this world, which is further from God every day, and which puts itself in the place of God and is destroying everything that is beautiful and good in the souls of each of you. Therefore, little children, arm yourselves **with prayer and fasting so that you may be conscious of how much God loves you and may carry out God's will.**

Thank you for having responded to my call.

May 25, 2010

Dear children! God gave you the grace to live and to defend all the good that is in you and around you, and to inspire others to be better and holier; **but Satan, too, does not sleep and through modernism diverts you and leads you to his way.** *Therefore, little children, in the love for my Immaculate Heart, love God above everything and live His commandments. In this way, your life will have meaning and peace will rule on earth. Thank you for having responded to my call.*

August 25, 2011

Dear children! Today I call you to pray and fast for my intentions, because Satan wants to destroy my plan. Here I began with this parish and invited the entire world. Many have responded, but there is an enormous number of those who do not want to hear or accept my call. **Therefore, you who have said 'yes', be strong and resolute.** *Thank you for having responded to my call.*

December 2, 2011 (to Mirjana)

Dear children! as a mother I am with you so that with my love, prayer and example I may help you to become a seed of the future, a seed that will grow into a firm tree and spread it's branches throughout the world. For you to become a seed of the future, a seed of love, implore the Father to forgive you your omissions up to now. **My children, only a pure heart,**

unburdened by sin, can open itself and only honest eyes can see the way by which I desire to lead you. *When you become aware of this, you will become aware of the love of God – it will be given to you. Then you will give it to others, as a seed of love. Thank you.*

January 2, 2012 (to Mirjana)

Dear children! As with motherly concern I look in your hearts, in them I see pain and suffering; I see a wounded past and an incessant search; I see my children who desire to be happy but do not know how. ***Open yourselves to the Father. That is the way to happiness, the way by which I desire to lead you.*** *God the Father never leaves His children alone, especially not in pain and despair. When you comprehend and accept this, you will be happy. Your search will end. You will love and you will not be afraid. Your life will be hope and truth which is my Son. Thank you. I implore you, pray for those whom my Son has chosen. Do not judge because you will all be judged.*

February 2, 2012 (to Mirjana)

Dear children! I am with you for so much time and already for so long I have been pointing you to God's presence and his infinite love, which I desire for all of you to come to know. And you, my children? You continue to be deaf and blind as you look at the world around you and do not want to see where it is going without my Son. You are renouncing him – and he is the source of all graces. ***You listen to me while I am speaking to you, but your hearts are closed and you are not hearing me. You are not praying to the Holy Spirit to illuminate you. My children, pride has come to rule. I am***

pointing out humility to you. *My children remember that only a humble soul shines with purity and beauty because it has come to know the love of God.* ***Only a humble soul becomes Heaven, because my Son is in it.*** *Thank you. Again I implore you to pray for those whom my Son has chosen – those are your shepherds.*

March 2, 2012 (to Mirjana)

Dear children! Through the immeasurable love of God I am coming among you and I am persistently calling you into the arms of my Son. With a motherly heart I am imploring you, my children, but I am also repeatedly warning you, that concern for those who have not come to know my Son be in the first place for you. Do not permit that by looking at you and your life, they are not overcome by a desire to come to know Him. ***Pray to the Holy Spirit for my Son to be impressed within you.*** *Pray that you can be apostles of the divine light in this time of darkness and hopelessness. This is a time of your trial. With a rosary in hand and love in the heart set out with me. I am leading you towards Easter in my Son. Pray for those whom my Son has chosen that they can always live through Him and in Him – the High Priest. Thank you.*

June 2, 2012 (to Mirjana)

Dear children! ***I am continuously among you because, with my endless love, I desire to show you the door of Heaven. I desire to tell you how it is opened: Through goodness, mercy, love and peace – through my Son.*** *Therefore, my children, do not waste time on vanities. Only knowledge of the love of my Son can save you. Through that salvific love and the Holy Spirit he chose me and I, together with him, am* *choosing you to be apostles of his love and will.* **My children, great is the responsibility upon you.** *I desire that by your example you help sinners regain their sight, enrich their poor souls and bring them back into my embrace. Therefore pray; pray, fast and confess regularly. If receiving my Son in the Eucharist is the center of your life, then do not be afraid, you can do everything. I am with you. Everyday I pray for the shepherds and I expect the same of you. Because, my children, without their guidance and strengthening through their blessing, you cannot do it. Thank you.*

July 2, 2012 (to Mirjana)

My children! Again, in a motherly way, I implore you to stop for a moment and to **reflect on yourselves and on the transience of this your earthly life. Then reflect on eternity and the eternal beatitude. What do you want?** *Which way do you want to set out on? The Father`s love sends me to be a* **Mediatrix** *for you, to show you with motherly love the way which leads to the purity of soul; a soul unburdened by sin; a soul that will come to know eternity. I am praying that the light of the love of my Son may illuminate you, so that you may triumph over weaknesses and come out of misery. You are my children and I desire for all of you to be on the way of salvation. Therefore, my children, gather around me that I may have you come to know the love of my Son and thus open the door of eternal beatitude. Pray as I do for your shepherds. Again I caution you: do not judge them, because my Son chose them. Thank you.*

July 25, 2012

Dear children! Today I call you to the 'good'. **Be carriers of peace and goodness in this world.** *Pray that God may give you the strength so that hope and pride may always reign in your heart and life because you are God's children and carriers of His hope to this world that is without joy in the heart, and is without a future, because it does not have its heart open to God who is your salvation. Thank you for having responded to my call.*

August 2, 2012 (to Mirjana)

Dear children! I am with you and I am not giving up. I desire to have you come to know my Son. I desire for my children to be with me in eternal life. I desire for you to feel the joy of peace and to have eternal salvation. I am praying that you may overcome human weaknesses. I am imploring my Son to give you pure hearts. My dear children, only pure hearts know how to carry a cross and know how to sacrifice for all those sinners who have offended the Heavenly Father and who, even today, offend Him, although they have not come to know Him. I am praying that you may come to know the light of true faith which comes only from prayer of pure hearts. It is then that all those who are near you will feel the love of my Son. Pray for those whom my Son has chosen to lead you on the way to salvation. May your mouth refrain from every judgment. Thank you.

Chapter 5
Medjugorje Our Lady Speaks To The World
CALLED TO WITNESS

As a result of experiencing the conversion power of Medjugorje, this book becomes another "fruit" in the evolution of the conversion experience. For with authentic conversion comes many changes, graces and gifts. In terms of logical thinking, if I had not experienced Medjugorje, there would not exist the three collections of music, nor the many music and message videos placed on YouTube for the world to see and hear. There would be no conversion story. I would not be married to Regina Marie, nor would I have two beautiful girls. I would not be aware of the messages of Our Lady and probably not living the messages as I am today. I would not have performed over 600 concerts as a witness to Medjugorje in and out of the U.S. God would not have influenced the lives that have been changed by saying "yes". I would not be writing this book and I would not have the peace I experience today.

As I look back, there was a point of transformation, a point of abrupt change, a point of conscious awareness that God was calling my life. That point in time is re-lived in my mind many times. I describe that single moment in time in my conversion story ***Medjugorje To the World – "Be converted."*** It came at the top of Mt. Krizevac at the foot of the thirteen ton cross, by the mystery of being led by the mysterious internal voice and the illumination of a simple directive **"I call you back to the faith of your youth, not**

for what you shall expect from it, but for what you shall now give to it." Everything that has followed from that point in time encompasses the infusion and influence of Medjugorje in my heart, mind and soul. For nearly 15 years, by invitation by the Holy Spirit I found myself witnessing to countless other lives in concert presentations and conference presentations. In early 2005, believing my mission was at an end, I resigned myself to the quiet living of small town America with my family. In continuing in the work of builder and developer, I lived content in the thought that I had followed to the best of my ability in serving what God and Our Lady had asked of me. I would continue to live the message of Medjugorje quietly and solemnly. It would not be for another four years that the mystical would break into my life again, and much to my surprise, with specific instructions.

It began in late fall 2008....

Vicki Martin, a hospice nurse and longtime friend from Des Moines, Iowa, called me to relay that one of her patients (Charlotte) at the hospice had mentioned she would be happy if she could hear Jerry Morin sing *The Lady of Medjugorje* to her one more time. I received the call on my answering machine and found the call to be a little confounding. I thought about the call that night and on the next day was prompted to call the hospice. I knew Charlotte. I knew she had attended one of my past concerts. I felt that God was leading me to make the call. The phone number was a direct line to Charlotte's private room. When she answered I started singing *O the Lady is calling*..... Charlotte started laughing and then we settled in to a very warm conversation. One of her comments to me was "I sure hope you don't have to stop singing." I realized very quickly, the following day, that I was glad I made the call, for Vicki called me to tell me Charlotte died early in the morning.

A couple days later, at the family's request, I drove to Des Moines to sing and play the *Ave Maria* on trumpet at the head of her casket at Mass. After Mass at the reception, Vicki and I and the bereaved family sat together. During our conversation Vicki asked how things were going. I explained I was busy with my work and I was confronted with a couple of real estate decisions, but I wasn't sure what I should be doing at this juncture of my life. She offered to pray for me. She suggested that, because I am a father and St. Joseph is the father of the Holy Family, that I should start a **Novena to St. Joseph** and not stop until I get an answer. I told her I would honor that request. She emailed the St. Joseph Novena to me and I began praying it in December of 2008. (You will find this Novena to St. Joseph at the end of this chapter.) Every day I would make time to pray the novena asking St. Joseph to intercede for me to God in helping me find the answer to what my life should be engaged in. On the **ninth day** of that novena I was led to read a small book on **<u>The Holy Will</u>**. It was one of only three books on the shelf that had been unpacked. I was so entranced in this reading that I read it in two nights. I recognized that I had never prayed a supplication to find God's Holy Will for my life. As days passed I was haunted with this Holy Will concept. I also realized, in reading this little book that the Holy Will was all that should matter to any spiritual life.

My wife was aware that through prayer I was intensely seeking the correct decision even though I was praying about real estate. My choices were:

1. Do I build one last home as our family home? We had purchased the land and had the blueprints.
2. Do I move a very nice home that the DOT (Department of Transportation) needed moving for a new highway bypass? (I had the experience of moving homes).

3. Do I do neither and discover something else more important?

The Holy Will began to affect the way I prayed. I was being shown more and more that this Holy Will was like finding the "great pearl", or the "great treasure in the field". I began to quietly surrender to this notion of the Holy Will, and I wondered if there was a discovery waiting for me. In essence, the Holy Will was a surrendering of my will to His Divine Will for my life. The book convinced me that I was being asked to pray for God's Divine Will and whatever that answer was, I believed it would lead to the most fulfilling experience of peace and joy. I recognized that the meaning of The Holy Will was the same that Our Lady was delivering in many of her messages: to surrender. The thought crossed my mind that possibly St. Joseph was leading me to ask for the Holy Will to be revealed for my life.

Regina then told me that she believed that Mary Immaculate Church was always open and suggested I should go there at night to pray where I would be away from the family noise and distraction. She said she had always received grace when praying in that church. I was surprised to discover that the church was open 24 hours.

I recall the first night I visited how quiet and incredibly peaceful I felt in the church. Here was Our Lady's large figured statue on one side, St Joseph on the other side and Jesus on the cross in front of me. Because I promised Vicki I would continue in the intercession of St. Joseph, I began frequenting the church each night with my St. Joseph prayers. In the first few visits to the church I discovered additional novenas to Saints Padre Pio, St. Therese of Lisieux, St Gerard, St Philomena (for my girls), St Raphael and St Gabriel. I also invoked intercession from Blessed Pope John

Paul II. I began to look forward every night to making my trek to the church. I would bring my little head lamp and sit there night after night, completely alone, to just sit and pray and experience the wonderful peace. I recall telling my wife I felt as if I was getting closer to my answer. I talked to Jesus and Mary a great deal in those evenings, speaking things to them from the recesses of my heart.

On one afternoon I had to attend to property responsibilities. I recalled Vicki asking if I ever listen to my own music. For my 90 mile drive I decided to take the *To The World I, II* and *III* CD's with me. On listening to the music I wept all the way down and all the way back. I recall asking myself over and over how could a person hear all that, be given all that? (For the previous four years I had absolutely no involvement with Medjugorje or the music). After having not heard the music for quite some time, the experience was like a gut wrenching hand reaching into the very recesses of my heart and pulling me in.

On my next visit to Mary Immaculate Church, I experienced a noticeable joy in my heart when invoking the saints to help

me in my earthly affairs. I continued praying to recognize the Holy Will for my life. That night I just wept uncontrollably at which time I was reminded of the conversion experience nearly 20 years ago in Medjugorje, and how these current experiences were having the same effect on me.

We were fast approaching the 2009 Lenten season when a very odd occurrence took place. I had no contact with anyone involved in Medjugorje for at least four years. In that period of time we had also moved three times due to my wife's position in Higher Education. I was on my way to drop my girls off at school when I received a call on my **CELL PHONE** from a Dianne Nason. She sounded frantic and weak. She felt it was a miracle that she found me. I remember thinking "You have no idea, honey, what a miracle it was you found me." Dianne was from Waterbury, Maine, and had just read my book, _To The World,_ in the Eucharistic Chapel. She felt compelled to locate me in seeking the _To The World_ music. I got her name and address and sent her a book and the three collections of music the following day. I recall thinking how very strange that call was, especially to my cell phone. I believed no one, outside of business relations and Vicki Martin, had my cell phone number. I immediately dismissed the call from my mind until I got home at supper and told my wife. She agreed it was a very strange call. On Ash Wednesday, after receiving ashes, I returned to the Mary Immaculate Church with the special novenas. My petition now shifted to discover God's Holy Will for my life. I believed God knew me better than I knew myself. If there was something more important I should be doing, it was time to know.

About 30 minutes into the novenas an internal hearing conveyed that **Mary would exchange her heart with me again**. That message proceeded to convey that all that was directed to me in Medjugorje many years ago would now be fulfilled, and that all I experienced before was in preparation for this time. I WAS STUNNED! I continued to listen attentively. The sensation, as if **God the Father** was speaking to me, was rapturing. I believed the Father was speaking about Mary and her messages and telling me **He needed me now at this time,** that my entire life was planned for this time.

Then I heard said **"YOU WILL NOW WITNESS TO THE WORLD, TO THE CHURCH AND TO THE VATICAN."** I felt like all time stopped. The sensation was that He needed me. The incredible awesome sense of being needed by God overwhelmed me emotionally. All kinds of questions came to mind and it seemed with every question there was an immediate answer.

I remember thinking or saying, "Why would you need me? Why would you need me now? I thought I was done?" I had already spent nearly 15 years of my life witnessing to the message of Medjugorje to the world and to the church. But what did **"TO THE VATICAN"** mean? Then I began to hear certain songs I had just listened to only a couple days earlier. This experience led immediately to internally viewing visuals accompanying the songs. I started intensely seeing videos…..music videos. It was then reiterated to me that not only was I not done, but everything that preceded was all in preparation for what I am now being called to fulfill. As I watched I began to see and understand **the music message videos**. Fighting the tears, I internally watched so many details of the music and videos and even various translations of the message videos. I was seemingly frozen in the viewing of all this. I recall clearly saying out loud in the church "You have got to be kidding me."

Many new things were now being introduced to me. There was a conveyance that Mary was very sad. She was sad in that many who were drawn near to her were quickly losing their way. The communication relayed that I was now being called to unify many of her children that were feeling lost, alone and **fractioned.** I would be leading many who would also be called out of their own personal deserts. With regularity and commitment **a mission** would be built, and people will recognize quote *"**all is in my de**sign**."** Then I heard "***The Servant*** song will help people to comprehend why the song was granted to you and what you mean to me."

I don't know how long the communication lasted. I was exhausted when done and in tears. At one point I asked "How will know this is from you and not some deception to disrupt my family?" The response was **"IT WOULD BE CONFIRMED MANY TIMES."**

I left the church late that night in total bewilderment. I was noticeably very quiet for the next several days, for even the thought of all this would bring me to tears every time. I had to ponder all of this quietly and search its meaning. I had so many questions. But as each hour of each day went by for the next few days it seemed that every question was being answered. I told Regina I had experienced something quite profound in the church, that I was trying to make sense of it, and it had nothing to do with real estate.

Being in the church on the following night, it started all over again- all the words, all the scenes- but then more was added. I was shown that being engaged in what was asked of me now was **The Father's Holy Will for my life.** It was not to build a house or move a house, but **The Father was asking me to build a mission** that would be in defense of His Mother's messages to the world, the Church and even the Vatican. Immediately, I was infused with the grace to understand what I was being asked. The mission was more than a request; it was a need on His Part. This awareness again created awe and great bewilderment. Why me? Why now?

The courage and power that was delivered to my heart and mind were unquestionable, and yet without any doubt, these were some of the most mystifying times of my life…just like the night in the St James Church in Medjugorje. These messages had the same intensity, same rapturing, same ecstasy, and the same hearing. On that particular evening I called Vicki Martin from the church and could barely talk. I conveyed to her almost word for word what I had just experienced. I told her I wasn't sure what I was supposed to do from here. I think she was in total awe at what I was conveying.

I often wondered how anyone could accomplish such a task even in a lifetime. Within a few days I then realized my response would again be a matter of faith and of seriousness. When asking again "Why me?" The answer I heard was **"*Why not you? I have given to you all of the gifts and tools and now you have my grace*"**. Many nights I wept. Everything that was presented to me brought a realization that all was a matter of faith and that again the courage and love to follow this would be granted to me. It would have been much easier to dismiss this as nonsense, but I had experienced being asked to trust and walk in faith before! It was a matter of faith and discernment. My love is great for Mary, but I wasn't sure how to respond to this. There were so many serious things to consider. With as much as I was experiencing, I felt it still was not enough to raise me from the spiritual desert.

Since I had not kept up with the current events of Medjugorje, I asked Vicki Martin if she had any updates. She explained she was a member of the International Internet Prayer Group *Queen of Peace* – an extension of Ivan, the visionary's prayer group. She proceeded to tell me that it was as dire a situation as ever, and that the spirit of oppression on all those involved with Medjugorje was palpable. Vicki was incredibly moved when I began to explain the Mary Immaculate experiences.

I proceeded slowly with these experiences. During the many nights of contemplation and prayer over all this, I was led to read another book of one of my favorite saints, St Therese of Lisieux. I also had completed a novena to her in the church. Regina and I both had witnessed St. Therese's intercessions in our personal lives, in our marriage and family. Those influences and intercessions can be read in the conversion story <u>Medjugorje to the World – "Be converted."</u>

Remember my bookshelf? Along with <u>THE HOLY WILL</u> and <u>DIVINE SURRENDER</u>, there set St. Therese's **STORY OF A SOUL**. The last time I read this book was approximately 20 years ago. I was so enthralled with reading every page that I read the complete book in one night. At the end of the book I discovered another novena to St. Therese. It was a unique **5-day novena** with specific instructions on praying it. It directed the reader to name your petition, and if it was in **God's Will** that He answer it, I would receive a rose on the 5th day (not the ninth day). On pondering this 5-day novena I was prompted to test the novena. <u>I decided that my petition would be directly related to the events experienced in the Mary Immaculate Church</u>. I also decided that I would write down inside a manila folder the date I would begin praying the novena and my petition. For some reason I felt it important to write this petition so it could be clearly read, especially in light of all that I was experiencing. I wrote the following: **"March 29, 2009. Start novena on the morning of the 29th before 11:00 a.m. I am testing the St. Therese Novena on this day."** I then wrote my petition which was in relation to the events experienced in the church.

I decided to write down a petition that I truly believed **only God could accomplish**. I prayed all five days of the novena. I recall on the morning of the 5th day as I was finishing the novena thinking that the probability of getting struck by lightning on this perfectly clear day was greater than receiving a rose.

At 6 p.m. of the 5th evening I retrieved the mail as I normally do and sat in my chair to open it. I came across an envelope that was unusual. I could barely read the return address, but I recognized the last name and Waterbury, Maine. I immediately called to Regina that this must be a *THANK YOU* note from the lady I sent the book and music. I opened up the envelope. There were two letters in the envelope, one to me and a carbon copy letter to Fr. Svetozar Kraljevic of Medjugorje. She had written previously to Fr. Svet to pray for her healing. Out of the letters dropped a holy card on my lap. When I looked down, I read the name **St. Therese** on the card. It took a few seconds for it to register, and then the idea of the final day of the novena hit me. I initially thought how odd. Then I turned the picture to the other side and I saw something totally unexpected: a **large relic rose petal on the other side**! I looked up in total awe and frantically called to Regina. She said, "What's wrong?" I asked her if she would read aloud the writing on the inside of the manila folder next to the chair. She asked "Why?" I asked her again to just read it aloud and I would explain. When she read it aloud she asked, "You have been doing this Novena?" I replied, "Yes, and this is the fifth day. Now look at this picture." She said, "Oh that's weird." Then I asked her to turn it over. She turned it over and then looked at me with surprise. I explained a great deal to her that evening. I told her I would have to somehow follow this and take some steps forward to see where it leads. Regina had witnessed a great deal, herself, in the last 20 years in our personal lives and with my apostolate. She had the faith to believe.

My Friends, this St. Therese confirmation that particular night, catapulted my faith and forced me to think about the written petition. At that very moment I felt the powerful hand of God pull me up. I would not be writing this story and re-publishing this book had it not been for this St. Therese and additional confirmations. I would like to share that it was several months later, while in Des Moines at Bill Kuhn's Studio working on the Power Point presentation for the Louisville Marian Conference, that we discovered several additional rose petals inside the envelope. ANOTHER CONFIRMATION!

That night I turned to the Scriptures. Recall what Paul said about Abraham in Romans chapter 4 vs. 20: *"He did not doubt God's promise in unbelief, rather he was empowered by faith and gave Glory to God and was fully convinced that what he had promised he was able to do."*

I believe Jesus revealed Himself to me in a very real way. It seemed that every random Scripture I turned to was speaking directly to me. I was led to key Scriptures about being a servant. I experienced Him speaking to my heart to be a servant, nothing more, nothing less. My chest felt like it was on fire. Then so much infusion of grace and understanding rushed into me. The Scriptures were never as alive to me as that night.

The greatest among you must be your servant. Whoever exalts himself will be humbled and whoever humbles himself shall be exalted.(Matthew 23:11)

Whoever serves Me must follow Me, and where I am there also will my servant be. (John 12:26)

Seek ye first the kingdom of heaven and all other things shall be added unto you. (Matthew 6:33)

Ask and you shall receive, knock and the door will be opened, seek and you shall find. (Matthew 7:7)

If you love me and keep my commands <u>My Father and I will come and make our home in you</u>. (John 14:21)

No one knows the Son except the Father and no one knows the Father except the Son and <u>ANYONE TO WHOM THE SON WISHES TO REVEAL HIM</u>. (Matthew 11:27)

Whoever has my commands and obeys them, he is the one

who loves me. He who loves me will be loved by my Father, and I will love him <u>AND SHOW MYSELF TO HIM.</u> (John 14:21)

Not everyone that says to me "Lord, Lord"……shall be saved, but he who keeps my commands <u>AND DOES THE WILL OF MY FATHER.</u> (Matthew 7:21)

These seemed immediate confirmations. The Holy Spirit's grace was totally encompassing in me.

The **following day** I called a friend on the East Coast who was always close to my earlier ministry. I felt prompted to call her to explain what had just happened. She immediately replied that this reminded her of an important Scripture that was shown to her that I should hear. It was **Habakkuk the Prophet**. She kept the scripture passage posted on her wall. I asked her to please read it to me. When she read it to me, I felt immediately that it was directed to me. On hearing it, my spirit was immediately lifted even higher in faith.

Then the Lord answered me and said: "Write down the vision clearly upon the tablets so that one can read it readily, for the vision still has its time, presses on to fulfillment and will not disappoint. If it delays, wait for it. It will surely come. It will not be late."(Habakkuk 2:2)

Only **HOURS** later, I retrieved my mail to find another letter from Dianne Nason of Waterbury. Maine. I was stunned to find the letter beginning with guess what? The exact words of the prophet Habakkuk, **the same Scripture verse referencing the vision**. I could hardly believe my eyes.

The confirmations do not cease and continue to this very day. Let me tell you sincerely, I believe I would not be communicating with you had not the St Therese confirmation taken place. That confirmation forced my mind to consider what I had written for the petition and has placed me in a state of awe ever since. The Habakkuk confirmation allowed me to keep hold of the vision. Now the confirmations support me in my faith and in my surrender to follow. Every time I begin to get a little anxious, my mind immediately moves to these powerful confirmations. I can only imagine what confirmations the early apostles witnessed. It is no wonder they were completely filled with the Holy Spirit! They were eye witnesses to Jesus's Resurrection and all the miracles.

Many of you are probably saying to yourself, "This is kind of heavy and serious." Yes, it is. We are in very serious times; this is not a time to be slack in the faith! This time is about our salvation; about our eternal life with God. As with any friend, you have to spend time together. To have God as your friend, you have to spend time with Him. We can experience the Kingdom of God right here in the here and now.

From the onset of the events at Mary Immaculate Church to the present, I have been in constant prayer and discernment and watchful for the holy impulses and confirmations. Silence and solitude have become my very good friends. In silence I am able to communicate with my God.

Another transformation that seemed to happen simultaneously is that I became very aware of my mortality. I am here to bloom for a little while and then gone. I have made a decision that while I have life and some bloom left, I surrender it to Them for Their designs. St Padre Pio said,

"How precious time is! Blessed are those who know how to make good use of it. Who can assure us that we will be alive tomorrow? Let us listen to the voice of our conscience, to the voice of the royal prophet: "Today if you hear His voice, harden not your heart." Let us not put off for one moment to another what we should do, because the next moment is not yet ours."

I now bring you up in time to the weekend of the Feast of Divine Mercy, March 25, 2012. I took this weekend opportunity to drive to Des Moines, Iowa, to share in the Divine Mercy celebration with friends. For me, this was a time of reflection and prayer and participation in one of my favorite devotions – Divine Mercy. On my 3-hour drive back home I had time to pray the Joyful, Sorrowful, Glorious and Luminous Mysteries of the Rosary. Within moments of their completion, I felt my mind "light up". I was stunned when the words **"WITNESS TO THE WORLD, THE CHURCH AND TO THE VATICAN"** were re-visited with a new illumination. It was being shown to me that <u>I was to present, as a witness to the conversion power of Medjugorje, all of the "fruits" of my works, and that I was to send these **"fruits"** as a **WITNESS** to the Vatican itself and the Sacred Congregation for the Doctrine of the Faith during this time of intense evaluation by the Vatican commission on Medjugorje.</u>

As I have related, my experience began in 2009, one year prior to Pope Benedict XVI appointing a new commission to study Mary's appearances at Medjugorje. These specialists were to report their findings to the Holy See by the end of 2012.

In midsummer, 2012, with the assistance of our spiritual director, Fr. Scott LeMaster, a package was sent to Cardinal

Ruini, head of the newly formed commission on Medjugorje. A separate package was mailed to His Holiness Pope Benedict XVI. Please understand, we may never know the outcome of this decision, but here is what I do know. I know that I have followed in faith what I believe is being asked of me, and that is sufficient to know for I believe this is His **Holy Will** that I follow.

As of the date of this publication over 24 music and message videos have been produced since the instructions I heard late that night in Mary Immaculate Church. These resources are available as English, German, and Italian message/music videos. They have been placed on YouTube and are accessible at www.servantstotheworld.com, Servants to the World Mission website. Over 40 countries, thus far, are currently viewing these videos. The English, German and Italian music message videos were also sent to Rome as part of the package. We all find it ironic that the only three languages we have recorded to date are these three languages, especially in light that Pope Benedict XVI is German and the Vatican is primarily Italian. The five message/music versions include *The Lady of Medjugorje, At The Cross, Live The Message, You're The Way* and *The Servant.*

As I follow this call, these words of St. Therese have been firmly planted in my mind and heart and are re-presented to me over and over:

"We have only these short moments to work for God's glory, the devil knows this, and that is why he tries to make us waste time in useless things."

I also draw upon the following words from Pope Urban VIII (1623-44) in this calling. His Holiness stated,

"In cases which concern private revelations, it is better to believe than not to believe, for if you believe, and it is proven true, you will be happy that you have believed, because our Holy Mother asked it. If you believe and it should be proven false, you will receive all blessings, as if it had been true, because you believed it to be true."

NOVENA TO ST. JOSEPH

Oh St. Joseph whose protection is so great, so strong, so prompt before the Throne of God, I place in you all my interests and desires.

Oh St. Joseph do assist me by your powerful intercession and obtain for me from your Divine Son all spiritual blessings through Jesus Christ, Our Lord; so that having engaged here below your Heavenly power I may offer my Thanksgiving and Homage to the Loving of Fathers.

Oh St. Joseph, I never weary contemplating you and Jesus asleep in your arms. I dare not approach while He reposes near your heart.

Press Him in my name and kiss His fine Head for me, and ask Him to return the kiss when I draw my dying breath.

St. Joseph, Patron of departing souls, pray for us. Amen

Say for nine consecutive mornings for anything you may desire. It has seldom been known to fail.

Chapter 6
Medjugorje Our Lady Speaks To The World

The Holy Will and Private Revelation

"Now there are varieties of gifts, but the same Spirit; and there are varieties of services, but the same Lord; and there are varieties of activities, but it is the same God who activates all of them in everyone. To each is given the manifestation of the Spirit for the common good. To one is given through the Spirit the utterance of wisdom, and to another the utterance of knowledge according to the same Spirit, to another faith by the same Spirit, to another gifts of healing by the one Spirit, to another the working of miracles, to another prophecy, to another the discernment of spirits, to another various kinds of tongues, to another the interpretation of tongues. All these are activated by one and the same Spirit, who allots to each one individually just as the Spirit chooses." (1 Cor. 12:4-11)

"Public revelation is binding on all Christians, but private revelation is binding only on those who receive it. The Catholic Church teaches that public revelation was completed, and therefore was concluded, with the death of the last apostle (Vatican II, Dei Verbum 4), **but private revelation has continued.**

"Throughout the ages, there have been so-called 'private' revelations, some of which have been recognized by the authority of the Church. They do not belong, however, to the deposit of faith. It is not their role to improve or complete

Christ's definitive revelation, but to help live more fully by it in a certain period of history. Guided by the Magisterium of the Church, the sensus fidelium [collective sense of the faithful] knows how to discern and welcome in these revelations whatever constitutes an authentic call of Christ or his saints to the Church. Christian faith cannot accept 'revelations' that claim to surpass or correct the revelation of which Christ is the fulfillment, as is the case in certain non-Christian religions and also in certain recent sects which base themselves on such 'revelations'" (Catechism of the Catholic Church 67). (1)

"St. John of the Cross, a Doctor of the Church and one of the greatest of mystic theologians, who had had so many special favors himself, is very severe with persons who desire to be the recipients of visions and revelations. He never wearies of repeating that the proximate means of union with God in this life is the three theological virtues of faith, hope, and love. True growth consists in intensified love, which is founded on faith and hope. Now although St. John encourages everyone to aim at infused contemplation, even though relatively few attain it, he strongly reproves anyone who desires to be the recipient of a vision or revelation. They desire to see; faith holds on without seeing.

St. Teresa of Avila, who herself had an abundance of visions, takes a similar stand. She admits that great profit can be had from such things when they are genuine and are received in the proper spirit. Yet she says (*Interior Castle* 6. 9): "I will only warn you that, when you learn or hear that God is granting souls these graces, you must never beg or desire Him to lead you by this road. Even if you think it is a very good one... there are certain reasons why such a course is not wise."

She then goes on at length to explain her reasons: First, such a desire shows a lack of humility; second, one thereby leaves self open to "great peril because the devil has only to see a door left a bit ajar to enter"; third, the danger of auto-suggestion: "When a person has a great desire for something, he convinces himself that he is seeing or hearing what he desires." Fourth, it is presumption for one to want to choose his own path, as only the Lord knows which path is best for us. Fifth, very heavy trials usually go with these favors: could we be sure of being able to bear them? Sixth, "you may well find that the very thing from which you had expected gain will bring you loss."

St. Teresa then adds that there are also other reasons, and continues with some wholesome advice that one can become very holy without this sort of thing: "There are many holy people who have never known what it is to receive a favor of this sort, and there are others who receive such favors even though they are not holy." We think of the frightening words of Our Lord in Mt. 7.22-23. Speaking of the last day, He said: ***"Many will say to me on that day: "Lord , Lord, did we not prophesy in your name, and cast out devils in your name, and work many miracles in your name? And then I will tell them: I never knew you. Depart from me you workers of iniquity."*** St. Teresa adds: "It is true that to have these favors must be a very great help towards attaining a high degree of perfection in the virtues; but one who has attained the virtues at the cost of his own work has earned much more merit.'"
(2)

On June 26, 2010 10:00 a.m. while in a state of raptured meditation, I received and wrote the following word for word on notebook paper. After a great deal of reflection and prayer, it is with courage and with love that I now share this:

"I desire that you teach the Holy Will. I desire that you illuminate to them the great importance of the Holy Will for their lives and to seek it. To all those who truly pray and seek it with all seriousness, I shall reveal it. To all those who truly pray and ask for it, I shall reveal it. To all those who pray and knock on heaven's door, even My saints are prepared to swiftly intercede on their behalf for Me to answer with it. Your access to the Kingdom of God exists here and now in the level of belief and faith in my Son; however, the discovery of the great pearl of My Holy Will for each life, and the surrender to it, ensures your salvation and eternal life with Me. Holy men and women, My servants throughout the ages, knew and comprehended this holy truth, and experienced the Kingdom of God in surrendering to it while they lived their lives on earth.

Tell them I make My Holy Will available for each life, but they have to want it and be prepared to surrender to it. If they only knew what surrender to My Holy Will means for life in the eternal, they would desire it more than anything in this world. I know the human heart and I know when they are serious to obtain it.

The importance of The Holy Will will become more and more important and illuminated in the conscious mind of man in these times before I manifest My power to the world. Those who live this Holy Will will be interiorly prepared to accept all to come without fear.

Your works and fruits produced in the living of The Holy Will are what I will accept and reward accordingly. My Holy Will can be discerned in those engagements and involvements that result in the fruit of Love and Charity from a Holy Spirit driven heart. All other works shall be consumed as hay, wood and rubble in the fire of non-existence."

....

Jesus said:

"All that belongs to the Father is Mine. That is why I said the Spirit will take from what is Mine and make it known to you. "I will take from what is Mine and make it known to you" (John 16:15)

Chapter 7
Medjugorje Our Lady Speaks To The World

Blessed John Paul II as Intercessor

In the **Called To Witness** chapter I mentioned seeking the intercession of Blessed John Paul II while praying in Mary Immaculate Church. Blessed Pope John Paul II will always have a special place in the hearts of many. He has a special place in my heart and here is why. For nearly six years my stepson, Nicholas, was ill. His second grade through seventh grade school years were very challenging, not only for him, but for our entire family. Nearly every morning Nicholas would wake up for school nauseated. This resulted in Nick spending his morning in the bathroom or in bed. The history of his condition evolved and involved more than 20 different physicians and specialists, 2 MRI's and 2 hospital stays in efforts to find the root cause of the chronic nausea. Medical bills were constant and the frustration and worry almost too much to bear, especially for Regina.

Nicholas's father was working for the advance team for the White House in preparing President Bill Clinton's greeting of Pope John Paul II's visit to St. Louis in 1999. Regina and Nicholas were presented with a special invitation to visit with the Pope privately with President Clinton. Regina felt a need to go with Nicholas. Regina had been praying for weeks to let Nick **"touch the hem of Your garment and be healed'** since conventional medicine was not finding a cause. Regina and Nicholas were blessed to shake Pope John Paul II's hand and kiss his ring during a private gathering at the St Louis Airport.

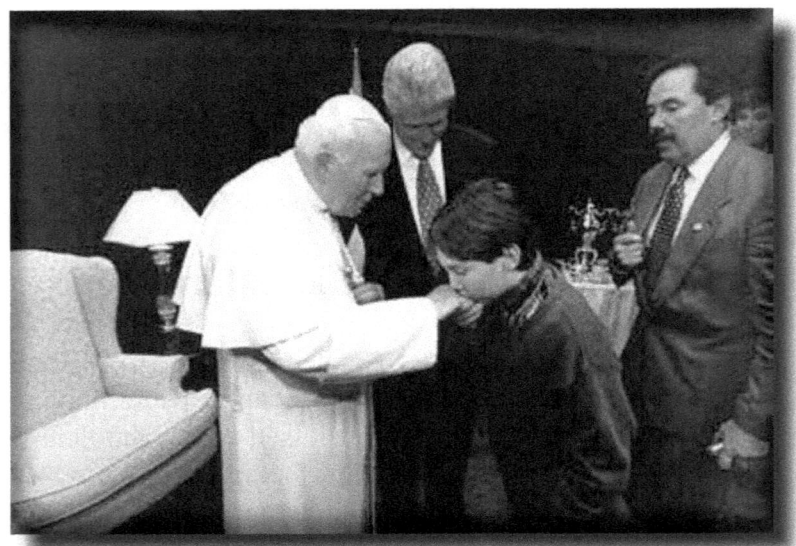

Nicholas with Pope John Paul II

Regina with Pope John Paul II

Within a week of that visit Regina was mysteriously led to find the cause of Nick's illness. The last medical specialist who had evaluated him was pediatric neurologist. He said it was a mystery, that it must be something autonomic causing the nausea, but he could not identify it. When Regina returned from the Pope's visit, she searched "autonomic" on the internet and found an entry from someone with the same symptoms as Nicholas. It turned out for that person that the chemical Aspartame, a chemical used in sugar substitutes, was the root cause. Regina also discovered that when Aspartame is heated it changes the chemical base. Regina immediately became aware of the possibility that the homemade tea that we drank every day included a sugar substitute that included Aspartame. When the basic tea was made, it was superheated in the microwave with the tea bags. Nicholas would drink a lot of this tea. As quickly as Regina chose not to use the particular sweetener, the changes with Nicholas's health seemed miraculous. The nausea and sickness subsided immediately. Nicholas was back to school full-time and felt fine. He eventually graduated from high school with highest honors. We all witnessed this and believe to this day that Nicholas **"touched the hem of His garment"** when he kissed Pope John Paul's hand.

A side story associated with Nick's healing is the fact that Regina shared the discovery with Nick's pediatrician, who additionally discovered the chemical was the source of her own chronic headaches. That physician believed it was miraculous that Regina discovered the source of Nick's illness.

Pope John Paul II, now Blessed John Paul II, and many times referred to as Our Lady's Pope, made many positive comments in Medjugorje. You will find several of his quotes in the **Facts and Quotes to Ponder** section at the end of the book.

Chapter 8
Medjugorje Our Lady Speaks To The World

Author's Reflection
On Fatima /Medjugorje

The events of Fatima captivated me from my earliest days of Catholic grade school. Fatima, with its secrets, has captured the attention and imagination of millions of people throughout the world. Many who have experienced Medjugorje have hypothesized, early on, that Medjugorje could possibly be an ongoing extension, or even possibly the fulfillment, of Fatima.

In June, 2000, the Vatican released the wording of the vision of the Third Secret of Fatima, stating that the Third Secret was fulfilled with the assassination attempt of Pope John Paul II in 1981. We read from the following words of Sister Lucia dos Santos, visionary of Fatima:

…."After the two parts which I have already explained, at the left of Our Lady and a little above, we saw an Angel with a flaming sword in his left hand; flashing, it gave out flames that looked as though they would set the world on fire; but they died out in contact with the splendor that Our Lady radiated towards him from her right hand: pointing to the earth with his right hand, the Angel cried out in a loud voice: Penance, Penance, Penance! And we saw in an immense light that is God: something similar to how people appear in a mirror when they pass in front of it a Bishop dressed in White we had the impression that it was the Holy Father. Other Bishops, Priests, men and

women Religious going up a steep mountain, at the top of which there was a big Cross of rough-hewn trunks as of a cork-tree with the bark; before reaching there the Holy Father passed through a big city half in ruins and half trembling with halting step, afflicted with pain and sorrow, he prayed for the souls of the corpses he met on his way; having reached the top of the mountain, on his knees at the foot of the big Cross he was killed by a group of soldiers who fired bullets and arrows at him, and in the same way there died one after another the other Bishops, Priests, men and women Religious, and various lay people of different ranks and positions. Beneath the two arms of the Cross there were two Angels each with a crystal aspersorium in his hand, in which they gathered up the blood of the Martyrs and with it sprinkled the souls that were making their way to God." (1)

According to documented sources, Sister Lucia continued receiving apparitions of The Blessed Virgin in the convent, some of which the Madonna mentioned her continued efforts in Medjugorje. (2) Pope John Paul II, himself, considered Medjugorje the fulfillment of Fatima.

It is believed, by many, that the description of the vision is not related to the shooting of Pope John Paul II, but describes more ominous portents related to the future of the Church, the Pope and the world. It is also believed, by many Fatima theologians, that there is more to the secret than has been revealed.

Antonio Socci, author of the <u>Fourth Secret</u> states:
"The Pope has now reopened the dossier of Fatima in such a precise and obvious way, that everyone, who, in the last years, had rushed to give praise to the official Curial version is now caught in panic by facing the Pope's words that place the pedophilia scandal within the Third Secret."(3)

In 2000, Cardinal Ratzinger (Pope Benedict XVI), as head of the Sacred Congregation for the Doctrine of the Faith, presented a Theological Commentary and was instrumental in the ratification of the *(official)* Vatican interpretation on the Third Secret of Fatima. (4) Ten years later, however, on May 13, 2010, Pope Benedict XVI resurrected the Third Secret in stating, *"We would be mistaken to think that Fatima's prophetic message is complete."* (5)

Could it be the Holy Pontiff has a deeper understanding of the meaning of Medjugorje and regrets his decision made in 2000? Could it be that His Holiness witnesses, from the chair of St. Peter, first hand, the rapid degradation of faith and morals in the world and in the Church? Does he view Fatima differently now? Does he view Medjugorje in light of Fatima? Does he agree with Pope John Paul II's words, *"Medjugorje, Medjugorje, it's the spiritual heart of the world"* and *"Medjugorje is the fulfillment of Fatima"* ?(6) Could it be, in his heart of hearts, he believes Our Lady has come to Medjugorje in unprecedented fashion and duration in Church history, and that he, alone, has the responsibility to the Mystical Body of Christ, as Supreme Pontiff and head of the Church, to give Mary as much support as possible? On March 17, 2010, The Holy See called for a new commission of specialists to study the events of Medjugorje. This commission is expected to report its findings to the Sacred Congregation for the Doctrine of the Faith and to His Holiness by the end of 2012. An announcement would be expected to be forthcoming.

On August 25, 1991, Mary's message at Medjugorje referred to Fatima: *"Dear Children... Therefore, I call all of you, dear children, to pray and fast still more firmly. I invite you to self-renunciation for nine days so that, with your help, everything that I desire to realize **through the*** *secrets I began in Fatima, may be fulfilled. I call you, dear children, to now grasp the importance of my coming and the seriousness of the situation. I want to save all souls and present them to God. Therefore, let us pray that everything I have begun be fully realized...."*

The great prophetess, Mary, at Medjugorje, comes to us as the "Queen of Peace." In one of her earliest messages she said: *"Peace is necessary for the salvation of the world."* Mary has, reportedly, presented over 30,000 messages. She continues her plea to the world for prayer, fasting, penance and conversion. On July 21, 1982, she illuminated many with the words, *"...Through fasting and prayer, one can stop wars, one can suspend the laws of nature..."* The world's hope and my hope is that the message of God, through Mary at Medjugorje, has the same outcome as the message of God sent through the prophet Jonah in the Old Testament. In Jonah 3:10, we read how Jonah was sent by God on a mission to the sin laden city of Nineveh with a message of impending destruction. Immediately the Ninevites began intense prayer and fasting. **"When God saw what they did and how they turned from their evil ways, he had compassion and did not bring upon them the destruction He had threatened."**

I have shared my reasons for re-publishing *Medjugorje To The World "Live The Message."*, now titled <u>*"MEDJUGORJE OUR LADY SPEAKS TO THE WORLD"*</u>. Beginning Ash Wednesday, 2009, I began a series of personal experiences throughout that Lenten season that, in essence, asked me to come forward at this time. **"WITNESS TO THE WORLD, TO THE CHURCH AND EVEN THE VATICAN."** This happened nearly a year prior to Pope Benedict XVI initiating a new international commission to study and report on Medjugorje. I surrendered to the fact that, if God has something here in these "fruits" of books and music He desires to use, I must try my best to respond and follow. Shortly after the onset of the personal experiences, I was invited to Louisville, Kentucky, to serve in the role of Master of Ceremonies at the Louisville Marian Conference. There, I also was presented with the opportunity to share my 2009 personal experiences, which subsequently led to my formation of the *Servants To The World* Mission. Two personal talks were recorded in Louisville that can be viewed on YouTube (links can be found in the Bibliography and Reference Sources). (7)

As a converted business man and believer in Our Lady's urgent message at Medjugorje, Mary's words brought the realization that my life was a pilgrimage here on earth. Remember Our Lady's message of March 25, 1988, "….. ***don't forget that your life is fleeting like a spring flower, which today is wondrously beautiful, but tomorrow has vanished….***" While I have a little bloom left, and if it is in His Will that I be a witness to Medjugorje, then as Our Lady said, *"Let it be done unto me."*

Every person is considered a child of God and a child of Mary, even the hardest of hearts and the greatest of sinners. In Matthew 9:12-13 Jesus said, ***"It is not the healthy who need a doctor, but the sick. But go and learn what this means: 'I desire mercy, not sacrifice.' For I have not come to call the righteous, but sinners."*** St. Bridget of Sweden said, **"There is no sinner in the world, however much he may be at enmity with God, who does not return to Him and recover His grace, if he has recourse to Mary and also her assistance."**

How appropriate it is that God would send Mary to Medjugorje on the Catholic Feast Day of St. John the Baptist,

June 24, 1981. This was the perfect representative feast day to symbolize repentance and conversion. Then on May 2, 1982, The Virgin Mary stunned many with these words: *"**I have come to call the world to conversion for the last time. Later, I will not appear any more on this earth.**"* Conversion is a very real experience and can be as sudden and dramatic as St. Paul being struck down off his horse with a blinding light or a gentle loving leading of Holy Spirit. Reconciling with God and neighbor are the first steps. Recite the Our Father slowly listening to every word in your heart. Seek forgiveness…. seek confession. Begin on the path of conversion and *"**pray! pray! pray!**"* Conversion is an ongoing process of mind, heart, and soul. If you are sincere and faithful to the grace of conversion, Jesus and Mary will light your path.

On May 13, 2010, His Holiness prayed to "hasten the fulfillment of the prophecy of the triumph of the Immaculate Heart". (8)

Let us take comfort in Our Lady's words at Fatima,

"In the end My Immaculate Heart will triumph."

Chapter 9
Medjugorje Our Lady Speaks To The World

Facts and Quotes to Ponder

1. **May 13, 1917** Our Lady of the Rosary first appeared to the three children of Fatima, Portugal, two girls and one boy. Our Lady revealed secrets at Fatima. She prophesied the end of World War I. She asked for the consecration of Russia to her Immaculate Heart. She requested Communion of Reparation on the First Saturdays. If her requests were not heeded a greater
war would result. *"Russia would spread her errors throughout the world, promoting wars and persecutions of the church; the good will be martyred, the Holy Father will have much to suffer, various nations will be annihilated.... in the end my Immaculate Heart shall triumph."*

2. **1939-1945** World War II begins as foretold by the Virgin Mary (estimated 60 million deaths)

3. **1959-1963** Coldest years of the Cold War (Russian/American relations at their worst)

4. **1960** Third part of the secret of Fatima not revealed by Pope John XXIII to the world as requested by the Virgin Mary at Fatima

5. **8/13/61** Border to West Berlin closed followed by the building of the Berlin Wall

6. **1962** Cuban Missile Crisis - the standoff between the US and Soviet Union - the closest the world came to nuclear war. Russian/American relations at a breaking point

7. **May 13, 1981** Pope John Paul II shot 4 times by assassin.

8. **1981** Pope John Paul II presented with the third part of the secret of Fatima after being shot.

9. **June 24, 1981** Blessed Virgin Mary reportedly begins appearing to six young visionaries, four girls and two boys in Medjugorje, Yugoslavia

10. **1981** Blessed Virgin reportedly conveys secrets to visionaries of Medjugorje

11. **May 13, 1982** Pope John Paul II visits Fatima to thank the Blessed Virgin for saving his life.

12. **May 13, 1982** According to testimony of the Medjugorje visionaries on the anniversary of the Fatima apparitions, and in regard to Pope John Paul II's Assassination attempt, Our Lady reportedly said: *"His enemies tried to kill him, but I have protected him."*

13. **1982** Pope John Paul II meets with visionary Sister Lucia, surviving visionary of Fatima.

14. **1984** Pope John Paul II publicly states to Bishop Pavel Hnilca: *"***Look, Medjugorje is a continuation, a veritable extension of Fatima***.*"

15. **1986** Pope John Paul II publicly states: **"If people are praying, fasting and being converted then let them go."**

16. **1987** Pope John Paul II in an interview with Mirjana Stated: **"If I weren't Pope, I would already be in Medjugorje confessing."**

17. **1988** Pope John Paul II states: **"Medjugorje! Medjugorje! Medjugorje! Only good things are happening at Medjugorje. People are praying there. People are going to Confession. People are adoring the Eucharist, and people are turning to God. And, only good things seem to be happening at Medjugorje."**

18. **1988** Pope John Paul II states to Bishop Murilo Krieger: **"Medjugorje, Medjugorje, it's the spiritual heart of the world."**

19. **August 1, 1989** Pope John Paul II publicly states: **"Today's world has lost its sense of the supernatural, but many are searching for it – and find it in Medjugorje, through prayer, penance, and fasting."**

20. 11/9/89 Fall of the Berlin Wall

21. **1990** Monsignor Angelo Kim when stating "Thanks to you, Poland was able to liberate itself from Communism", the Holy Father responded **"No, this is not my merit. This is the work of the Blessed Virgin Mary as she had predicted in Fatima and in Medjugorje."**

22. **April 8, 1992** Mother Teresa conveys: **"We are all praying one Hail Mary before Mass to Our Lady of Medjugorje."**

23. Pope John Paul II states to Monsignor Murilo Sebastiao Ramos Krieger, Archbishop of Florianopolis in Brazil, **"Medjugorje is the spiritual center of the world."**

24. **6/21/2000** Third secret announced as officially fulfilled with assassination attempt of Pope John Paul II. Authenticity of content met with skepticism and doubt by many. Theological Commentary delivered by Cardinal Ratzinger (Pope Benedict XVI).

25. **5/13/2010** Pope Benedict XVI resurrects Third Secret of Fatima. He states, **"We would be mistaken to think that Fatima's prophetic message is complete***."*

26. **5/17/2010** Pope Benedict XVI calls for International Commission of specialists to study and report on Medjugorje by year end 2012.

27. **2012** Our Lady continues to appear and deliver messages to Medjugorje visionaries.

MEDJUGORJE UPDATES
New Vatican Commission

On March 17, 2010, His Holiness Pope Benedict XVI called for a new commission to study and report its findings to the Congregation for the Doctrine of the Faith at The Holy See by the end of 2012 or early 2013.

"Press office of The Holy See reported on Wednesday, March 17th, that The Holy See, as a part of Congregation for the Doctrine of the Faith, established International Commission that will be investigating phenomenon of Medjugorje. Camillo Ruini is the Chairman of Commission that was made of cardinals, bishops and experts. During the press conference in Vatican, Fr. Federico Lombardi, Director of The Holy See Press Office, explained that mentioned Commission will be operating with full discretion, and that all results that will follow after long term operation, will be delivered to Congregation for the Doctrine of the Faith. Archbishop Allessandro D'Errico, Apostolic Nuncio to Bosnia and Herzegovina, gave this information to bishops of Bishop's Conference of Bosnia and Herzegovina, as instructed by Cardinal Secretary of State, Tarcisio Bertone." (1)

UPDATE ON VISIONARIES (2)
" Vicka Ivankovic-Mijatovic

Vicka is the oldest of the visionaries and was born on September 3, 1964, in Bijakovici. She comes from a family of 8 children. Her prayer mission given to her by Our Lady is to pray for the sick. Our Lady appeared to her for the first time on June 24, 1981. For her, the daily apparitions have not yet stopped. Our Lady so far has confided nine secrets to her. Vicka married on January 26, 2002, and lives with her husband Mario in the small village of Gradac, a few 180 kilometers north of Medjugorje. They have two children Sophia Maria, and Anton.

Ivan Dragicevic

Ivan is the older of the two boys who see Our Lady and was born on May 25, 1965, in Bijakovici. His prayer mission given by Our Lady is to pray for priests, families, and the youth of the world. Although Ivan and Mirjana share the same last name, they are not related. Our Lady has appeared to him every day since June 24, 1981. Our Lady has confided nine secrets to Ivan. He is now married and resides half the year in the parish of Medjugorje, and half the year in Boston, MA. Ivan and his wife Laureen have four children.

Mirjana Dragicevic-Soldo

Mirjana was born March 18, 1965, in Sarajevo. Her prayer mission from Our Lady is to pray for all unbelievers. She is the second oldest of the seers. Very intelligent, Mirjana graduated from the University of Sarajevo where her family lived. Mirjana was the second to see the Blessed Mother that day, June 24 in Medjugorje. She had daily apparitions from June 24, 1981, till December 25, 1982. On this date, Mirjana received her 10th and final secret from Our Lady. Mirjana was the first seer to receive all 10 secrets. Since that time, Our Lady only appeared to Mirjana once a year on her birthday (March 18) until August 2, 1987, when Our Lady also started appearing to Mirjana on the second day of each month to pray with Mirjana for all unbelievers. Mirjana tells us that Our Lady defines "unbelievers" as those who have not yet felt God's love. She tells us that if we only once saw the tears in Our Lady's eyes for all unbelievers that we would all begin praying intensely for this intention. Mirjana lives in Medjugorje with her husband Marko Soldo. They have two daughters.

Ivanka Ivankovic-Elez

Ivanka was the first to see Our Lady on June 24, 1981, and is the youngest of the 4 girls and was born on July 21, 1966, in Bijakovici. Ivanka's prayer mission from Our Lady is to pray for families. She had daily apparitions from June 24, 1981, until May 7, 1985. On that day Our Lady confided to her the last of her ten secrets. Our Lady told her that for her entire life she will have an apparition every year on June 25, the anniversary of the apparitions. And so far it has been just that way. Ivanka is living in the parish of Medjugorje, is married and has three children.

Jakov Colo

Jakov is the youngest of the seers. He was born on March 6, 1971, in Bijakovici, and was only 10 years old when the apparitions started. His prayer mission given by Our Lady is to pray for the sick. He has had daily apparitions since June 25, 1981, and on September 12, 1998, Our Lady confided to him his tenth secret. Our Lady now appears to Jakov only once per year on Christmas Day.

Marija Pavlovic-Lunetti

Marija is the third oldest of the visionaries. She was born on April 1, 1965, in Bijakovici. Her prayer mission given by Our Lady is to pray for all the souls in purgatory. She has three brothers and two sisters. When the apparitions started, she was studying in Mostar which is about eighteen miles away from Medjugorje. Our Lady appeared to her for the first time on June 25, 1981. She still has apparitions every day and is the visionary to whom Our Lady gives the public message to the world on the 25th of each month. Our Lady has confided nine secrets to her so far. Marija is presently living in Italy, is married, and has four children. She visits Medjugorje a number of times each year."

About the Author

Immaculate Conception Grade School- Fitchburg, Massachusetts

Notre Dame High School- Fitchburg, Massachusetts

Fitchburg State College-- BS Biology

Professional singer/songwriter/musician in show band (The Prodigy) and own band (Revelation) entertaining audiences throughout the country for 7 years

Commercial Broker--- Builder--- Developer (30 + years)

Profound conversion experience (November 1988)

Founder of Respond Ministry-- Lay Apostolate (1989)

Author/ Composer ***To the World I, II & III*** music collections

Author of ***<u>Medjugorje To the World - "Be converted"</u>*** and ***<u>Medjugorje Our Lady Speaks To The World</u>***

Three separate occasions as guest on Mother Angelica's Eternal Word Television Network

Conference speaker and concert presenter 1989 through 2010, nationally and internationally

Sponsored and directed 1992 Heartland Marian Conference, Des Moines, Iowa

Husband and father of two daughters and two stepsons

Columbia College- BA Business

Columbia College- MBA

Profound Second Call during Lenten season 2009 - Founder of *Servants to the World* Mission (Lay Apostolate) *www.servantstotheworld.com*

"Seeking and fulfilling God's will is my only objective while I have life on this earth."

-Jerry Morin

SERVANTS TO THE WORLD MISSION

A profound personal vision and accompanying instructions has revealed that the Servants To The World Mission, formed in 2009 as a result of a *second call* will be extended throughout the world. I am being asked to follow and obey Their instructions. God has shown to me, in unexpected fashion, that the words first received in Medjugorje over twenty years ago will now be fulfilled. His plan incorporates all of Our Lady's children worldwide.

As of the date of this writing, Servants To The World Mission, in its infant stage, is being observed in its saturation of the entire world. Over 40 countries are viewing our music and message video productions on YouTube. What was only a personal vision during the Lenten season of 2009 has already manifested itself into reality. I can only pray that Their purpose for this mission is fulfilled completely, according to God's Holy Will.

We and Our Lady encourage and invite her servants, with open arms, to join with us in God's plan for the world with this mission. We are witnesses and all have a role to play as Servants To The World Mission unfolds.

-Jerry Morin
A servant in the mission

Author's "Fruits" of Medjugorje

"Make a tree good and its fruit will be good, or make a tree bad and its fruit will be bad, for a tree is recognized by its fruit." (Matthew 12:33)

"By their fruit you will recognize them." (Matthew 7:6)

Medjugorje To The World I music collection CD (*The Lady of Medjugorje, The Servant, Lovely Lovely Lady*)
ISBN 978-0-9663280-8-0

Medjugorje To The World II music collection CD *(Live The Message, At The Cross, Say Yes, You're My Lady)*
ISBN 978-0-9663280-9-7

Medjugorje to The World III *music collection CD (Let Them Know The Reasons, The Power of God. Proclaim My Name)*
ISBN 978-0-9857464-0-7

Queen of Peace Messages To The World (Audio CD). Our Lady's messages with voice and *To The World* background instrumental tracks.
ISBN 978-0-9857464-1-4

Medjugorje To The World – "Be converted" The conversion power of Medjugorje is demonstrated in Jerry Morin's remarkable story with reflection on Fatima/Medjugorje connection. Epilogue graciously written by Fr. Petar Ljubicic – the priest chosen by the visionaries to reveal the secrets, beforehand, at the appointed time.
ISBN 978-0-9663280-1-1

Medjugorje To The World – "Be converted"
AUDIOBOOK personally narrated by author Jerry Morin. Actual song soundtracks in place of song lyrics. Female voice Regina Morin
ISBN 978-0-9663280-5-9

Medjugorje To The World – "Be converted" Same book with **accompanying AUDIOBOOK (combo).**
ISBN 978-0-9663280-4-2

Medjugorje To The World – "Be converted" Same book with **accompanying** *Medjugorje To the World I* **CD.**
ISBN 978-0-9663280-3-5

Medjugorje Our Lady Speaks To The World - Book with early years synopsis of Medjugorje with Scripture and Reflection. Author shares personal call and reflects on Fatima/Medjugorje connection
ISBN 978-0-9663280-2-8

Medjugorje Our Lady Speaks To The World Same book with **accompanying** *Queen of Peace Messages To The World* **audio CD.**
ISBN 978-0-9663280-7-3

Medjugorje Our Lady Speaks To The World **AUDIOBOOK** Narrated by Jerry Morin and accompanying Queen of Peace messages spoken by Regina Morin
ISBN 978-0-9857464-6-9

Medjugorje Our Lady Speaks To The World BOOK AND AUDIOBOOK (combo)
ISBN 978-0-9857464-7-6

**Please join us at *www.servantstotheworld.com*
and present your witness to the world with us.**

You can find these "**Fruits**" **of the author** on Amazon.com, Kindle, Nook, local Catholic and Christian bookstores and *www.medjugorjetotheworld.com*

Bibliography & Endnotes

Before Our Eyes-the Virgin Mary Zeitun Egypt. Pearl Zaki. Queenship Publishing, © 2002.

Quotable Saints. Ronda De Sola Chervin. Servant Publications, © 1991.

Butler's Lives of the Saints, Four Volumes, edited and revised and supplemented by Herbert J. Thurston, S.J. and Donald Attwater (Westminster, Maryland; Christian Classics 1956).

To The World – Live The Message. Jerry Morin; Respond Ministry, © 1989.

In The Company of Mary. Fr. Svetozar Kraljevic. Franciscan Herald Press, Chicago, Illinois, 1988.

The Apparitions of Our Lady at Medjugorje. Fr. Svetozar Kraljevic. Franciscan Herald Press, Chicago, Illinois, 1984.

Catechism of the Catholic Church. Excerpts from the English translation for use in the United States of America, © 1994, United States Catholic Conference, Inc. – Liberia Editrice Vaticana. Used by permission.

Mother of Christ Crusade. Free booklet published 1947 Fall River, MA.

Medjugorje and the Church. Denis Nolan. Queenship Publishing Co., 1995.

St. Therese of the Child Jesus. EDITIONS DE L'OFFICE CENTRAL, ST. RUE du Carmel, LISIEUX (Calvados) France, Printed at the Printing Press of the Master Printer Draeger Brothers at Paris, May 17, 1955.

The New American Bible. Catholic Book Publishing Co. New York © 1970 by the Confraternity Of Christian Doctrine, Washington, D.C., including the revised New Testament, © 1986.

HOLY BIBLE, NEW INTERNATIONAL VERSION, ©
1973, 1978, 1984 by International Bible Society. Used by
permission of Zondervan. All rights reserved.
Messages of Medjugorje.Respond Ministry Marian Center.
Messages from www.medjugorje.eu/messages
Messages from www.medjugorje.ws/en/messages
Picture of St Therese of Lisieux – used with royalty paid
permission – www.dreamstime.com
St. Joseph Novena Prayer from PIETA PRAYER BOOK
Publishers and Copyright Owners - Miraculous Lady of
Roses, LLC, PO Box 111,Hickory Corners, MI 49060

Approved Apparitions –

1. Pg. VII http://campus.udayton.edu/mary/resources/aprtable.html

www.miraclehunter.com

The Holy Will and Private Revelation

1. PG 112 *http://www.catholic.com/tracts/private-revelation*
2. Pg 113 *http://www.ewtn.com/faith/teachings/maryd8.htm*

Facts and Quotes to Ponder

1. http://www.vatican.va/roman_curia/congregations/cfaith/documents/rc_con_cfaith_doc_20000626_message-fatima_en.html http://www.fatima.org/essentials/facts/popeapprov.asp
2. http://en.wikipedia.org/wiki/World_War_II
3. http://www.americanprogress.org/issues/2008/09/cold_war_lessons.html
4. http://www.vatican.va/roman_curia/congregations/cfaith/documents/rc_con_cfaith_doc_20000626_message-fatima_en.html
5. http://en.wikipedia.org/wiki/Cold_War,Berlin_Crisis_of_1961. http://en.wikipedia.org/wiki/Cold_War
6. Bay_of_Pigs_Invasion_and_the_Cuban_Missile_Crisis
7. http://en.wikipedia.org/wiki/Pope_John_Paul_II_assassination_attempt
8. http://www.vatican.va/roman_curia/congregations/cfaith/documents/rc_con_cfaith_doc_20000626_message-fatima_en.html
9. http://www.medjugorje.eu/messages/
10. http://www.medjugorje.eu/messages/
11. Crossing the Threshold of Hope, by Pope John Paul II." Published by Alfrede A. Knopf, Inc. distributed by Random House, Inc., New York, 1998
12. Daniel Klimek, March 13, 2010 – http://www.ministryvalues.com
13. http://www.sister-lucia.excerptsofinri.com/
14. http://www.medjugorje.hr/en/news/mons.-pavel-m%C3%A1ria-hnilica,-s.j.-has-died,1297.html
15. By Daniel Klimek, March 13, 2010 – http://www.ministryvalues.com
16. http://www.spiritdaily.net/Medjtripstory.htm

17. http://www.spiritdaily.net/minnesotabishopmedjugorje.htm
18. Daniel Klimek, March 13, 2010 – http://www.ministryvalues.com
19. Daniel Klimek, March 13, 2010 – http://www.ministryvalues.com
20. http://www.dailysoft.com/berlinwall/history/fall-of-berlinwall.htm
21. Daniel Klimek, March 13, 2010 – http://www.ministryvalues.com
22. <u>Medjugorje, What Does The Church Say?</u>, Sister Emmanuel Maillard and Denis Nolan, Queenship Publishing Jan 1, 1998
23. http://www.medjugorjemiracles.com/2011/06/conclusive-proof-that-pope-john-paul-ii-believed-in-medjugorje/
24. <u>http://www.vatican.va/roman_curia/congregations/cfaith/documents/rc_con_cfaith_doc_20000626_message-fatima_en.html</u>
25. <u>http://www.cfnews.org/b16-3rd-sec.htm</u>. Article Pope Resurrects Third Secret – John Vennari, 2010
26. <u>www.catholic.org</u>. Article - Vatican Announces Members of Medjugorje Commission 4/13/2010
27. http://www.medjugorje.ws/en/updates/

Medjugorje Updates

1. www.medjugorje.org. March 25, 2010 Article – *HOLY SEE ESTABLISHED INTERNATIONAL COMMISSION FOR MEDJUGORJE*2. www.medjugorge.org Article - *About the Visionaries*

Author's Reflection on Fatima/Medjugorje

1. http://www.vatican.va/roman_curia/congregations/cfaith/documents/rc_con_cfaith_doc_20000626_message-fatima_en.html - *The Message of Fatima*
2. Medjugorje, Triumph of the Heart – Sister Emmanuel Maillard – Queenship Publishing, 2004
3. The Fourth Secret of Fatima – Antonio Socci – Loreto Publications July 13, 2009 and http://www.fatimaperspectives.com/ts/perspective 527.asp - Article - *The Truth Breaks Out in Italy* – Christopher A. Ferrara
4. http://www.cfnews.org/b16-3rd-sec.htm. Article *Pope Resurrects Third Secret* – John Vennari, 2010
5. http://www.cfnews.org/b16-3rd-sec.htm. Article *Pope Resurrects Third Secret* – John Vennari, 2010
6. http://www.medjugorje.org/wordpress/archives/33 Article - *Pope John Paul II "Medjugorje – The Spiritual Heart of the World"* By Daniel Klimek, March 13, 2010 – http://www.ministryvalues.com
7. Louisville Marian Conference 2010 – Jerry Morin Conference Talk 1 - http://youtube/xG0absr7Q60
Jerry Morin Conference Talk 2 - http://youtube/gaREDnzuFmA
8. http://www.cfnews.org/b16-3rd-sec.htm. Article *Pope Resurrects Third Secret* – John Vennari, 2010

Servants To The World Publications P.O. Box 642 Kirksville, MO 63501. Email: publisher@servantstotheworld.com

www.ingramcontent.com/pod-product-compliance
Lightning Source LLC
Chambersburg PA
CBHW061439040426
42450CB00007B/1129